197

22.⁰⁰

US
and
THEM

A HISTORY OF INTOLERANCE IN AMERICA

US
and
THEM

A HISTORY OF INTOLERANCE IN AMERICA

JIM CARNES

Preface by Justice Harry A. Blackmun

Illustrations by Herbert Tauss

OXFORD UNIVERSITY PRESS

NEW YORK • OXFORD

Contents

Oxford University Press

Oxford   New York
Athens Auckland Bangkok Bombay
Calcutta Cape Town Dar es Salaam
Delhi Florence Hong Kong Istanbul
Karachi Kuala Lumpur Madras Madrid
Melbourne Mexico City Nairobi
Paris Singapore Taipei Tokyo Toronto
and associated companies in
Berlin   Ibadan

Published by Oxford University Press, Inc.,
198 Madison Avenue
New York, New York 10016

Oxford is a registered trademark of
Oxford University Press

Library of Congress
Cataloging-in-Publication Data

Carnes, Jim.
   Us and them : a history of intolerance
in America / by Jim Carnes ; with illustrations by Herbert Tauss.
      p.   cm.
   Includes bibliographical references
and index.
   ISBN 0-19-510378-5 (library ed.)
   1. Prejudices—United States—
History—Juvenile literature. 2. Fanati-
cism—United States—History—Juvenile
literature. 3. United States—Race relations—Juvenile literature. 4. United
States—Ethnic relations—Juvenile literature. I. Tauss, Herbert, ill. II. Title.
E184.A1C335 1995
305.8'00973—dc20   95-11367
                                          CIP

1 3 5 7 9 8 6 4 2

Printed in Hong Kong
on acid-free paper

Preface

Why are we so willing not to accept others who are not precisely like us? Why do racism and anti-Semitism, for example, run so deep in the consciousness of many Americans? Is it because of man's basic inhumanity to man, or is it prompted by a sense of inferiority that makes us want to dominate others, to protect our turf, and to seek a status with no competition? Our country's otherwise glorious history is stained with instances of intolerance and hate. Intolerance, it seems to me, is taught and is not inherent in man's character. It is taught at a young age by overprotective elders, by unfortunate examples, and by poor-mouthing differences rather than exulting in the excitement of their presence. Childhood and the teen years are periods where diversity leads to discovery and, in the process, teaches. If that process is denied, we learn less and the stranglehold of ignorance breeds suspicion.

Us and Them vividly demonstrates what we have done—and are doing—to ourselves in ways antithetical to what is fair and good, to what is right by any standard, to good manners, and, indeed, in its ultimate conclusion, to peace in the world. It is time that we recognize intolerance for its miserable worth and, at last, work together to eliminate it. This will be a difficult task, but it is a difficult task worth doing. In *Us and Them,* Jim Carnes shows us the magnitude of the problem and the profound hazard in con-tinuing to ignore it.

One last word: Diversity yields strength. This is America's history and example. Indeed, diversity is our very creed, as is evident from the wording of our Constitution and its Amendments, from our persistent acknowledgment of the equality of persons, and from our accepting each other and profiting from our differences. To oppose it is to ignore and violate the American testament and its precious dream.

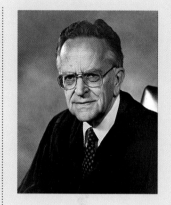

—Justice Harry A. Blackmun

Introduction

This book tells the stories of some Americans who were hated by others simply for who they were, what they looked like, where they came from or what they believed. Their experiences form a part of our history that is painful to read and think about, one that many of us might prefer to ignore. But it is only by examining the failures of the American experiment that we earn the right to celebrate its triumphs.

The founders of our nation outlined the principles of democracy in words that speak for all of us. The Declaration of Independence asserts: "We hold these truths to be self-evident, that all men are created equal." The opening phrases of the Constitution proclaim that "We the people" seek a "more perfect union." The Bill of Rights spells out the basic freedoms guaranteed to all Americans.

Yet the experience of many individuals shows that these universal principles have not been universally applied. The equality declared in 1776 belonged, in fact, to white men — not to men of other races, nor even to white women. The same Constitution that established our democratic government turned a blind eye to slavery. It also failed to prevent the United States from seizing the ancient homelands of native tribes. "We the people" clearly did not include everyone.

This narrow view of American-ness reveals a common truth about the way most of us view ourselves and others. We derive a large portion of our identity from the groups we belong to. Our family, our school, our team, our side of town, our party, our country, our religion, our race, our language — all of these are different ways of saying "us." And for every "us" and "ours," there are "them" and "theirs."

One group's attitude toward others often becomes ingrained. Each generation teaches the next one who the enemy is. Before the first European settlers reached American shores, they had heard wild tales about the "savages" they would find here. Systematic injustice toward African Americans lingered long after slavery had been abolished. In 1913, the campaign by Georgians to convict Leo Frank for a crime he didn't commit reflected the ancient practice of scapegoating Jews. In our own time, simply being "different" can make a young gay man like Charlie Howard the object of hate.

These stories and others like them are recounted in this volume. Consider them "flashlight views" into some of our nation's shadows. Perhaps in their power to unsettle and even unnerve us,

they can serve as cautionary tales. As you read them, you'll begin to see how easy it is for people to divide the world into "us" and "them." You'll learn about some of the deep-seated causes of prejudice and bigotry, and you'll come to recognize some of the rationalizations used to defend these attitudes.

You may be surprised to discover that some groups who are now full participants in American society faced hostility when they first arrived. "In the City of Brotherly Love" concerns a clash between native-born Protestants and Irish Catholics in Philadelphia in 1844. In this story, you'll find that many of the same stereotypes heard about immigrants today were used 150 years ago. And if you read "A Rumbling in the Mines," about an attack on Chinese laborers in Wyoming in 1885, you'll see that group hatred often originates from economic insecurity. None of this means, of course, that a complex issue like immigration can be reduced to a simple equation, but exploring its history may help you meet the challenges it poses for the future.

Because these stories depict such extreme confrontations, you may conclude that they are not particularly relevant to your own life. In fact, the intolerance described here arose from the fear and suspicion and anger of ordinary people — the same kinds of feelings we see expressed around us every day. Ethnic jokes, anti-gay graffiti, barriers to the handicapped — even the smallest denial of a person's rights and dignity can plant the seeds of injustice and hate.

Public opinion polls and the daily headlines make it plain: Around the country, many Americans — and, increasingly, young Americans — are drawing bolder lines between "us" and "them." The rise in hate crimes is the most visible and shocking sign of this trend.

It is easy to be pessimistic, to assume that things will never change. But the promise of America has always been larger than the reality. Over the course of two centuries, our collective experience has broadened our understanding of the proposition that "all men are created equal." Today our laws and our public institutions more justly — if not yet fully — recognize the equality of all people.

In a sense, our history can be read as a struggle to embrace the full measure of who "We the people" are. Time and again, Americans once excluded from the circle have claimed their birthright in the old ideals. In so doing, they have made us all fuller beneficiaries of our nation's creed. They have kept us moving, slowly but surely, toward a "more perfect union."

Above. The Declaration of Independence was signed in Independence Hall, Philadelphia, on July 4, 1776.

The Silencing of Mary Dyer

The early colonists in Massachusetts Bay managed to escape religious oppression in England only to be confronted by a new brand of tyranny: a church whose leaders governed both their public and private lives. In the 17th century, the Puritan Church was the law, and anyone who dissented from its orders was punished without mercy.

Like the other principles enshrined in our Bill of Rights, the separation of religion from government was not easily won. For Mary Dyer, it was an idea worth dying for.

ARY DYER LEFT ENGLAND in 1635 an outlaw — a Puritan whose religious faith was declared illegal by the national Church of England. Rather than change her religion, she, along with many others, chose to leave her home and start a new life on the strange and distant shore of Massachusetts Bay. It was the kind of choice Mary would face again and again, and her decision each time would be the same. Her faith came first — even if it meant her death.

So much about life in the young Bay Colony was unknown and fearsome. Half of the first 700 colonists died of scurvy within the first two years. Crude heating in wooden buildings caused frequent fires. Men took their guns to church with them in case of Indian attack. Members of the colony relied on each other's labor and loyalty simply to survive. They found courage in their common faith and depended on the Church to keep that faith in focus.

The hardships of her new life only made

"The Cursed Sect of the Quakers"

The General Laws and Liberties of the Massachusets Colony, issued in 1672, included an anti-Quaker provision.

Whereas there is a pernicious Sect, commonly called Quakers, ... whose Actions tend to undermine the Authority of Civil Government as also to destroy the Order of the Churches, ... they have not been deterred from their impetuous Attempts to undermine our peace and hasten our ruine;

For prevention thereof, This Court doth Order and Enact, that every person or persons of the cursed Sect of the Quakers, who is not an Inhabitant of, but found within this Jurisdiction, shall ... come before the next Magistrate, who shall commit the said person or persons to close Prison, there to remain without Baile until the next Court of Assistants where they shall have a legal trial by a special Jury, and being convicted to be of the Sect of the Quakers, shall be sentenced to Banishment upon pain of Death.

Mary's faith stronger. As she sought a deeper understanding of God's plan for her, she came to believe that God spoke to every person, including herself, through the urgings of his or her conscience. It was this belief — that all people had free access to God's truth — that led Mary and her husband, William, to doubt some of their church's teachings.

The Puritan Church governed all aspects of life in the colony. Church leaders dictated what people could wear and how they should behave, both in public and inside the home. The Old Testament was the foundation of civil law. Anyone convicted of violating one of the Ten Commandments was punished by hanging. Anyone who questioned the official faith was treated as a criminal. Women in Massachusetts were not even allowed to discuss a sermon, much less voice their own ideas about religion. Mary and William soon recognized in their own church and government the same intolerant spirit that had driven them out of England.

For as long as she could, Mary maintained an uneasy silence, in keeping with church rules. And then she heard another woman speak.

The women of the Dyers' neighborhood — in what is now downtown Boston

— gathered regularly to share certain chores, such as weaving and soap-making and gardening. And to share their thoughts. The neighbor Mary Dyer grew closest to was Anne Hutchinson. To the astonishment of her peers, Anne openly opposed the rigid authority of the church leaders. She believed that no church had the authority to govern a society. In her view, God spoke to everyone, male and female, and gave each individual the ability to discern right from wrong. Hearing Anne say these things out loud filled Mary with both relief and excitement, as if her own mind had suddenly been freed from a cage.

Anne Hutchinson organized a weekly religious meeting, which Mary Dyer faithfully attended. The swelling crowd soon included members of the clergy and the local government. Anne's eloquence and her knowledge of the Bible impressed everyone who heard her. Her popularity continued to grow until John Winthrop himself set out to stop her.

A respected Puritan minister, Winthrop was elected the Colony's first governor in 1631 and eventually served 12 annual terms in the position. In 1637, after his

own congregation turned to Hutchinson for spiritual guidance, Winthrop brought charges of slander against her in the general court. Many of her followers abruptly turned away from her. At the trial, she was banished from the colony. Knowing that the same thing could happen to her, Mary Dyer stepped to the front of the courtroom to take her friend's hand. For Mary, there was no choice. She had risked her

life before for the right to practice her faith, and she would do it again.

The new ideas that Anne and Mary and their friends had been spreading didn't just make Gov. Winthrop angry — they made him afraid. Amid so much physical uncertainty, Winthrop believed that a united spirit among the colonists was essential for their common survival. He feared that a loosening of Church control would endanger not only the colony's welfare but also its charter from the King. Division and controversy were the Devil's business. When word came that Anne Hutchinson and her family had been killed by Indians on Long Island, Winthrop proclaimed it the work of the Lord.

In Anne's absence, Mary vowed to continue the struggle that her friend had begun, no matter what the consequences. She followed her conscience in defying the law and speaking out about her own convictions. Everyone, she said, had the right to believe and practice religion as he or she saw fit. William Dyer tried to work within the government to get the laws on religion changed. In response to their efforts, a court banished Mary and William from the Bay Colony in 1638. They moved to Rhode Island and helped to found the settlement of Newport, where their six children were born.

Women in Massachusetts were not even allowed to discuss a sermon, much less voice their own ideas about religion.

Thanks to the leadership of Roger Williams, the colony's founder, residents of Rhode Island enjoyed a religious freedom that did not exist in Massachusetts. Still, even in this liberal atmosphere, Mary Dyer felt that something was missing: the voices of women. Rhode Island's independent churches were still run exclusively by men. Like her friend Anne Hutchinson, Mary viewed the separation of Church and State as a principle worth dying for, and one whose benefits should encompass all people.

On a trip to England around 1650, Mary met George Fox, the founder of the Quakers. Fox shared Mary's belief that the Puritans

Opposite page, above.
Fear of Indian raids prompted the Puritans to post guards during church services.

Left, above and below.
The "scourging," or public whipping, of Quakers was a common practice in Massachusetts Bay.

"Their Own Judgments and Consciences"

In its royal charter of 1663, the Rhode Island Colony became the first government in history to guarantee religious freedom to every citizen.

No person within the said colony, at any time hereafter shall be any wise molested, punished, disquieted, or called in question, for any differences in opinion in matters of religion. ... All and every person and persons may, from time to time, and at all times hereafter, freely and fully have and enjoy his and their own judgments and consciences, in matters of religious concernments, throughout the tract of land hereafter mentioned.

hadn't gone far enough in reforming Christianity. They had rejected the rituals and other remnants of Catholicism that they saw in the Church of England, but they had left all authority in the hands of a few. Like Mary Dyer, George Fox believed that God's revelation was freely available to every individual. He made his way from town to town, encouraging men and women to preach.

Mary followed where her spiritual path was leading her. She became a Quaker and stayed away in England for seven years.

During this time, John Endecott, the new governor of the Massachusetts Bay Colony, was having his own trouble with people like Mary Dyer. Quakers had recently begun coming over from England to spread their radical ideas. They walked into Puritan church services and denounced the preachers. They told people to listen for the voice of God inside them. To Gov. Endecott and his fellow churchmen, this was not just heresy — it was blasphemy.

The Quakers also defied the law. They didn't approve of war, so they refused to serve in the militia. It was against their belief to take oaths. On the street, Quaker men declined to tip their hats to the magistrates and other government officials. They said they only saw fit to bare their heads when they prayed.

To the Puritan leaders, such open defiance of authority indicated a desire and intention to tear down the government. Gov. Endecott authorized a law requiring that all Quakers be banished from the Colony, all Quaker books burned, and any Quaker arriving from England placed in jail.

Mary Dyer hadn't heard about the law when she decided to return to America, but as her ship sailed into Boston Harbor in 1656, she knew that life as she remembered it would never be the same. She and William still loved each other, but they had been apart a long time. The older children were grown now. And the sense of purpose that she had found on her journey was stronger than anything she'd ever felt before.

Captains of vessels sailing from England were required to put a 'Q' beside the names of all Quakers on their passenger lists. This made it easy for authorities to arrest unwanted arrivals. (A later law set a steep fine for even transporting them.) Mary Dyer was taken to prison as soon as she stepped ashore. William didn't know his wife was back in the colonies until several months later when a messenger delivered a note asking him to come and get her. William brought her back to Rhode Island.

While Mary stayed in Newport with her family, the situation in Boston kept getting worse. As the Quakers became more defiant, Gov. Endecott instituted harsher laws. Now any man who declared himself a

IN CONTEXT

Witch Hunting

Puritan intolerance reached a frenzied extreme in 1692. In May of that year, the daughters of a Puritan minister in Salem Village, Mass., began behaving in wild and unpredictable ways. One of them tried to burn herself in the fireplace. Rev. Samuel Parris soon learned that his household slave, a West Indian woman named Tituba, had been telling the girls stories of voodoo and witchcraft from her native islands.

First the Parris sisters claimed that they were possessed by the Devil themselves. Then they accused Tituba and three other Salem Village women of witchcraft. The charges caused a sensation, and within a few months a kind of "witch fever" had spread across eastern Massachusetts.

Civil authorities, with the support of Puritan ministers, appointed three judges to a special court for trying the accused witches. Witnesses were permitted to offer "spectral evidence," or descriptions of foul deeds they had seen performed by spirits. The list of suspects at one point included the wife of Gov. William Phips. As a result of the witch trials, 13 women and six men were hanged. One man was sentenced to death by "pressing" with heavy weights. Three women died in jail, along with an

Quaker would have an ear cut off. If he refused either to leave the colony or to abandon Quakerism, he lost the other ear. Women received whippings for their first two offenses. The crime of blasphemy could get a person's forehead branded with the letter 'B.' Puritan officials pierced the tongues of some Quakers with hot irons to prevent them from speaking out any more.

Not even these extreme measures seemed to work. Quakers from the other colonies kept coming to support their brethren. Mary Dyer walked all the way up from Newport to visit kindred spirits in jail.

unnamed infant belonging to one of the women who was executed.

The suffering brought on by the witch hysteria eventually turned public opinion against the trials. Families of the victims called for the colonial legislature to restore their loved one's reputations and to withdraw the orders that had denied their civil rights. Such a bill, also authorizing damage payments, was passed in 1711.

The Salem witch trials demonstrated that in an environment of widespread suspicion and intolerance, it only takes a spark to cause a wildfire. The memory of that episode is evident today in the phrase "witch hunt," which has come to mean any investigation that plays on a community's fear of unpopular ideas.

The most famous modern "witch hunt" was the crusade launched by U.S. Sen. Joseph McCarthy of Wisconsin in 1950 to rid the government of individuals he con-

sidered to be traitors. McCarthy offered no evidence for his claim that he had identified 205 communists in the State Department. But the prominence of his own office caused many Americans to believe him.

McCarthy's unfounded accusations of treason ruined hundreds of careers and made him, for a time, one of the most powerful figures in government. None of the charges was ever proved. His targets also included any individuals in civil service suspected of being homosexuals.

In 1954, after McCarthy was unable to get one of his assistants excused from the draft, he retaliated by "investigating" the military. Television broadcasts of the Army-McCarthy hearings exposed the Senator's cruel and unethical tactics to the public. Later that year, the Senate formally condemned McCarthy's conduct.

Above. The first time Mary Dyer was led to the gallows, she saw her two companions hanged.

Left. Puritan authorities arrest an old woman on charges of witchcraft.

Gov. Endecott saw no way around it: He announced that any Quaker entering Massachusetts Bay Colony would be put to death.

On her third venture to Boston, in 1659, Mary Dyer and two friends, Marmaduke Stephenson and William Robinson, were arrested and tried for their religious beliefs. They were given two days to leave the commonwealth, or else face the gallows. Mary went to Newport for a short time but returned and was seized.

Mary's son William traveled to Boston and convinced Gov. Endecott to withdraw her death sentence. Mary had already climbed the steps to the gallows when young William appeared on horseback. "Reprieve! Reprieve!" he shouted.

Although the Governor had granted Mary amnesty, she was ordered to stand with the rope around her neck, her feet and hands still tied, while her two companions were executed.

The fire of her convictions now burned even stronger in Mary's mind. She lived in the freedom and comfort of Rhode Island for a year but was not content. She decided to return to Boston, prepared to accept the consequences. She was promptly arrested and jailed.

Gov. Endecott came to visit Mary in prison. He tried to talk her into giving up her religion. Instead, she wrote letters to government officials insisting that they were the ones who ought to change.

Mary's hanging was scheduled for June 1, 1660, on Boston Common. This village green was a mile's walk from the prison. Fearing that Mary would preach to the crowds along the way, the Governor stationed all his troops — about 200 men — on horseback up and down the street. He ordered the militia drummers to drown out anyone who tried to speak.

The crowds broke through. People had come from all over the district to witness the spectacle. "Don't go!" they called out. "Go

Below. Many Quakers departed the Massachusetts Bay Colony to seek religious freedom.

back to Rhode Island. Go back and live!" The drums got louder.

Mary's guards escorted her across the Common to an elm tree next to Frog Pond. Standing there was Pastor Wilson, who had baptized her first child many years earlier. He begged her to save herself, to give up the ideas that had brought her to death's door.

She calmly refused, adding that she looked forward to life beyond the grave.

She climbed the ladder. Pastor Wilson loaned the hangman his handkerchief to cover her face. Mary Dyer did not protest her fate.

She remained silent as the ladder was pulled out from under her.

The crowd stood a long time without stirring.

"She hangs like a flag," someone said.

After he had removed the ladder, Edward Wanton, the hangman, walked over and vomited into Frog Pond. He went home and told his mother he had quit his job.

"I have met the most beautiful woman in the world," he said, "And now I'm going to become a Quaker." ◆

No Place to Pray

Many people have come to America seeking religious freedom. The Puritans did so, then promptly placed restrictions on religious practice in their own colony. Quaker Mary Dyer and others objected and paid with their lives. Eventually, as our nation of immigrants became more diverse, dozens of faiths found their place in the American patchwork.

Even though the Bill of Rights guaranteed freedom of religion, a number of groups have suffered persecution for their beliefs. Many Native Americans, for example, were forced to abandon their traditional religions, and only recently have some tribes won the right to follow the old ways. The religion commonly known as Mormonism originated in the United States, but its followers faced violence and exile before they found a home where they could live in peace.

Jews, Catholics, Muslims, Hindus, Sikhs, evangelical Christians — almost every religious group has experienced some form of intolerance. And yet, systematic persecution of religious groups in American history is relatively rare. One group who became victims of organized intolerance were the Hutterites.

In the 1870s, a group of German Christians known as Hutterites began immigrating into the northern Great Plains. For more than 300 years, the Hutterites had endured intolerance in Europe. Now they hoped to establish their agricultural "colonies" on the open prairie and live in peace.

Neighboring farmers quickly became suspicious of the newcomers. At that time, it was not so unusual that the Hutterites spoke German or wore plain clothes. But the fact that they lived communally — rejecting the idea of private property — was another matter. And so was their disregard for the outside world.

That world erupted in war in 1914, and the U.S. entered the conflict three years later. The Hutterites numbered nearly 2,000, spread among 17 colonies in South Dakota and two in Montana. As pacifists, the Hutterites had no use for the Liberty Bonds their neighbors were buying to support the U.S. Army. As these same neighbors sent sons off to fight the German Kaiser's troops, the Hutterites refused.

In the name of patriotism, farmers vandalized Hutterite buildings and raided the colonies' herds. Ordinances were passed to limit the use of German on the telephone and in schools and other assemblies. Some young Hutterite men were arrested for evading the draft. A court sentenced three brothers in the Hofer family to 20 years in the federal prison at Alcatraz, in San Francisco Bay. They were later moved to Fort Leavenworth, Kan. John and Michael Hofer died there as a result of physical abuse. Before sending the bodies back to South Dakota for burial, prison officials dressed one of the brothers in a military uniform.

South Dakota conducted an investigation of the Hutterites during this period. The State Council of Defence called the Hutterite communal organization "un-American" and recommended dissolving the colonies. Courts declared that the colonies were not religious bodies but corporations operating for economic gain. The application of corporate property laws forced most of the Hutterites to leave for Canada.

Blankets for the Dead

The Native American tribes uprooted by white settlement and expansion are too numerous to name. For many years, Indians were simply driven back by armed violence or the threat of violence. Then, in 1830, the government began systematically removing all Native Americans from the Eastern U.S.

The removal of the Cherokees from Georgia in 1838 has become known as the Trail of Tears. But there were, in fact, many such trails, as the Creeks, Choctaws, Chickasaws, Seminoles and other tribes were forced to abandon their homelands.

FOR MORE THAN A CENTURY, the Cherokees had watched first the colonies and then the United States chip away at their old tribal territory. In treaty after treaty, they exchanged one more piece of land for one more promise of respect and coexistence.

The Cherokees, like most Eastern tribes, sided with the British during the Revolutionary War because they feared that an independent American republic would take over their land. Shortly after the war, their fears deepened as the new government claimed all of the remaining Cherokee portions of North and South Carolina and part of those in Tennessee. Shrunken, subjected to constant harassment, in the early 1800s the Cherokee Nation adopted a new strategy for survival.

The tribe already counted among its number many British traders and soldiers who over the years had married Cherokee women. Now the Indians began to adopt the ways of white outsiders. Many took up Christianity. They began to replace their small stick-and-wattle

"A Country More Suitable"

Government treaties with the Indians claimed that removal was in the Indians' best interest.

The Seminole Indians [regard] with just respect the solicitude manifested by the President of the United States for the improvement of their condition, by recommending a removal to a country more suitable to their habits and wants than the one they at present occupy in the territory of Florida.
— *U.S. Treaty with Seminoles, 1832*

The Choctaw people, now that they have ceded their lands, are solicitous to get to their new homes as early as possible, and accordingly they wish that a party may be permitted to proceed this fall to ascertain whereabouts will be most advantageous for their people to be located.
— *U.S. Treaty with Choctaws, 1832*

The Chickasaw nation find themselves oppressed in their present situation .... Being ignorant of the language and laws of the white man, they cannot understand or obey them. Rather than submit to this great evil, they prefer to seek a home in the west, where they may live and be governed by their own laws.
— *U.S. Treaty with Chickasaws, 1833*

houses with large structures made of logs, lumber or bricks. Textile makers wove cotton and wool cloth to use at home or sell in general stores.

Schoolchildren practiced their arithmetic and learned to read in both English and Cherokee. (The invention of an alphabet by a half-Cherokee, half-white man named Sequoyah brought the Cherokee language into written form.) Cherokee farmers tilled the rich earth of the valleys using foreign methods and equipment, just as whites planted Indian crops. Some wealthy Cherokee landowners even purchased black slaves.

In 1827 the Cherokee Nation adopted a constitution based on that of the United States. The following year, a bilingual newspaper called *The Cherokee Phoenix* became the first Native American voice in U.S. journalism.

The Cherokees' efforts to coexist didn't prevent some frontier whites from trying to steal their property. Ironically, most of those who harassed the Indians couldn't read the English section of the Cherokee newspaper.

A Congressman from Georgia perpetuated the image of the Cherokee "savage" by publicly declaring that the Indians of his state lived on a crude diet of roots and reptiles. During a Washington dinner party, a visiting Cherokee leader made a point of

Andrew Jackson, who had risen to fame by waging wars against the Creek Indians in Alabama and the Seminoles in Florida, won the presidency in 1828 on a campaign promise of free land for white settlers. Jackson promoted the idea (first proposed by Thomas Jefferson) of moving Indians into unsettled prairie west of the Mississippi to make room for whites. In mid-May 1830, Congress gave Jackson his wish by passing the Indian Removal Act. The law set a new course for Indian/white relations. No longer did the government pretend to desire peaceful coexistence within its borders.

The Choctaws of Mississippi were the first Southeastern tribe to be removed to the West. The Creeks of Alabama and the Chickasaws of Mississippi and Tennessee were relocated next. Beginning in 1835, the Seminoles in Florida fought off the U.S. Army for seven years before finally giving up their homeland.

The Cherokees knew their turn was coming. They knew about the sufferings of the

> *The majority of whites still regarded Cherokees as ignorant and inferior.*

asking the legislator to pass "those roots" — by which he meant the potatoes. In this case, it could be said that "savagery" was in the eye of the beholder.

The Cherokees had transformed their culture in a single generation, in hopes of proving their humanity to their white neighbors and gaining the right to live undisturbed. Still, when it came to changing the government's attitude toward Indians, cultural transformation wasn't enough. Despite the outward signs of equality, the majority of whites still regarded Cherokees as ignorant and inferior. This prejudice was heightened by greed: Whites craved Indian land for themselves. And, in Georgia in 1828, the discovery of gold made that land even more desirable.

Far left. The surrender of Creek Chief William Weatherford to Gen. Andrew Jackson in 1814 ended the bloody Creek War and ceded vast tracts of Indian land in Alabama and Georgia to the U.S. government.

Left. Sequoyah's daughter Anyokah helped him develop the Cherokee writing system around 1820.

other tribes. But the Cherokees had kept their faith in "civilization." In 1832, they had appealed to the U.S. Supreme Court and won the right to remain independent and self-governing.

This right existed only on paper. The State of Georgia ignored it, as did Pres. Jackson. Federal agents, armed with ready cash, found a small group of Cherokees willing to sign a removal treaty. In December 1835, the Treaty of New Echota turned over to the U.S. government all that was left of the Cherokee lands (about 35,000 square miles in the region where Georgia, Tennessee and North Carolina meet) in exchange for $5 million and a parcel of western prairie.

The vast majority of Cherokees rejected the arrangement and stayed put while its supporters joined a small fragment of the tribe already living in the west. The Cherokees had played by all the rules, but the government kept changing them.

Among the influential whites who spoke out against Indian removal were Davy Crockett and Daniel Webster. But their influence couldn't turn the tide. White squatters interpreted the treaty as permission to seize Indian land. To complete the process, Jackson's hand-picked presidential successor, Martin Van Buren, mobilized an army to evict the Indians.

On a warm week in May 1838, into the peaceful north Georgia towns and farms of the Cherokees marched 7,000 U.S. soldiers. Their orders came directly from the president: Herd every Cherokee man, woman and child off the land.

The commander of this army, Gen. Winfield Scott, asked the Cherokees to cooperate so that his soldiers would not have to resort to physical force or violence. He asked them to help him make the best of a terrible situation. But Scott's vision of an orderly evacuation could not hold. Across Cherokee country, men were ordered at gunpoint from their plows, women from their looms. Jubilant whites looted or burned or occupied the homes left behind.

The experience had been similar for other tribes. One Choctaw elder never forgot the day he and his family were driven from their comfortable Mississippi homeplace: A 5-year-old, he was playing in the front yard when men

Cherokee Alphabet.

(chart of Cherokee syllabary characters)

Sounds represented by Vowels.

a, as a in *father*, or short as a in *rival*   o, as aw in *law*, or short as o in *not*.
e, as a in *hate*, or short as e in *met*   u, as oo in *fool*, or short as u in *pull*
i, as i in *pique*, or short as i in *pit*   v, as u in *but*, nasalized.

Consonant Sounds

g nearly as in English, but approaching to k. d nearly as in English, but approaching came with a wagon and ordered everyone to get in. The strangers made him leave his toys in the dirt, and by the time the wagon pulled out, a white boy — the son of the new household — was already playing with them.

There was little resistance to the Cherokee roundup after all. Although several hundred tribe members escaped into the remote mountains of North Carolina (where their descendants still live today), 15,000 others were held in 13 makeshift concentration camps in North Carolina, Georgia, Tennessee and Alabama until the massive removal to the West could be organized.

For a few of the Cherokees, the difficult 800-mile journey by river and over land began immediately after they were taken captive. The government hired local businessmen along the way to provide the exiles with food, clothing and transportation. These contractors were often willing to endanger Indian lives for the sake of extra profit. Spoiled meat and flour caused widespread sickness. Poor maintenance of riverboats made drownings commonplace. Many Indians preferred to walk rather than board the "death ships."

A summer drought halted river travel and forced most of the Cherokees to wait in the camps, which amounted to wilderness prisons. Diseases like cholera and

IN CONTEXT

Savages

In 1828 — the same year *The Cherokee Phoenix* began publication — Noah Webster issued his *American Dictionary of the English Language*. This was the first new dictionary produced in the United States, and in it we find the following definition:

SAVAGE, n. A human being in his native state of rudeness; one who is untaught, uncivilized or without cultivation of mind or manners. The savages of America, when uncorrupted by the vices of civilized men, are remarkable for their hospitality to strangers, and for their truth, fidelity and gratitude to their friends, but implacably cruel and revengeful towards their enemies.

Behind the irony of Webster's example lurk the mixed feelings that many white Americans held toward the Indians. On the one hand, the idea of the "noble savage" had been around since the ancient Greeks. It became especially popular in Europe during the 18th and 19th centuries, when science began to challenge many religious assumptions.

According to this view, American Indians, like the native inhabitants of

Africa and the Pacific Islands, represented humanity in its original state. Rather than blind souls lost in darkness, noble savages were seen as being good by nature (hospitable, truthful, faithful and grateful, in the words of Webster) because civilization had not yet taught them to be otherwise.

In sharp contrast to this romantic image, however, was the "cruel and revengeful" strain that many whites saw in the Indian character. The possibility that the policies or actions of white settlers were in any way to blame for the hostility they encountered among the natives was too disturbing for most to admit. It was much more convenient to regard Indians as fundamentally different from — and inferior to — whites. Thomas Jefferson could acknowledge the humanity of Indians in theory. But treating them as equals would have challenged his vision of an expanding United States.

Since white settlers couldn't afford to see a reasonable cause for Indian violence, they used this violence to justify their own. Indian resistance only strengthened their resolve to rid the land of what they considered a physical and moral danger.

This vicious circle of reasoning caused whites to commit deeds that belied their own claims to "civilization."

Making Room

In 1830, Pres. Andrew Jackson outlined for Congress his reasons for supporting Indian removal.

Philanthropy could not wish to see this continent restored to the condition in which it was found by our forefathers. What good man would prefer a country covered with forests and ranged by a few thousand savages to our extensive Republic, studded with cities, towns, and prosperous farms, … occupied by more than 12,000,000 happy people, and filled with all the blessings of liberty, civilization, and religion?

The present policy of the Government is but a continuation of the same progressive change by a milder process. The tribes which occupied the countries now constituting the Eastern States were annihilated or have melted away to make room for the whites.

Three years later, Pres. Jackson made his point even plainer:

That those tribes can not exist surrounded by our settlements and in continual contact with our citizens is certain. They have neither the intelligence, the industry, the moral habits, nor the desire of improvement which are essential to any favorable change in their condition.

Letter from a Choctaw Chief

In his 1832 "Letter to the American People," Choctaw Chief George W. Harkins sought to expose the deception and manipulation behind the government's Indian policy.

It is said that our present movements are our own voluntary acts — such is not the case. We found ourselves like a benighted stranger, following false guides, until he was surrounded on every side, with fire or water. The fire was certain destruction, and a feeble hope was left him of escaping by water. A distant view of the opposite shore encourages the hope; to remain would be inevitable annihilation. Who would hesitate, or who would say that his plunging into the water was his own voluntary act? Painful in the extreme is the mandate of our expulsion. We regret that it should proceed from the mouth of our professed friend, and for whom our blood was commingled with that of his bravest warriors, on the field of danger and death.

But such is the instability of professions. The man who said that he would plant a stake and draw a line around us, that never should be passed, was the first to say he could not guard that line, and drew

(Continued on page 21)

dysentery spread quickly because of the oppressive heat and overcrowding. Many Cherokees died before the journey had really begun.

In October, the remaining 13,000 Cherokee men, women and children in the camps were ordered to gather what belongings they could carry and begin moving West, under the guard of U.S. Army soldiers. Autumn rains had made the rivers navigable again but reduced the roads to quagmires. Cold weather brought new epidemics of whooping cough and measles. The travelers marked every stopping place with new graves. In places where the ground was frozen or there wasn't enough time for burial, they covered the bodies of the dead with blankets.

Other tribes faced the same difficulties. The Seminoles still commemorate a similar experience. To this day, at Seminole funerals, a new blanket is spread over the coffin to symbolize the hardships the ancestors endured during the Removal.

A government agent described the Choctaws' ordeal, as well as his own moral conflict: "They are a wretched set of beings, nearly naked, and have marched the last twenty-four hours through sleet and snow, barefooted. If I could have done it with propriety, I would have given them shoes."

Soldiers who took pity on the Indians and tried to help them could be punished for their actions. In the winter of 1832, a boat loaded with Choctaws got stuck in ice on the Arkansas River near Fort Smith. The lieutenant escorting the party requested extra blankets from the boat's supply. Without them, the stranded Choctaws faced death from exposure. When a superior officer denied the request, the lieutenant physically attacked him in order to get the blankets released. For this attempt to aid the Indians, the lieutenant was dishonorably discharged from the Army.

All told, nearly 100,000 Indians from the five Southeastern tribes walked into exile during the 1830s. More than 4,000 Cherokees, or a quarter of the tribe, perished on the journey. The Creeks and Seminoles suffered even heavier losses. The Seminoles mounted the strongest resistance

to removal, but by 1858, after repeated battles with U.S. forces, barely a hundred of them remained in Florida.

For the survivors of the Trails of Tears, the opportunity to "prosper and be happy," which the treaties had promised, proved an elusive dream. But the sense of tribal identity remained strong. Today, a sacred fire made from coals carried by Cherokee women from their homeland in 1838 still burns near Gore, Okla.

The great Indian removals didn't solve the "Indian problem." They only postponed it. Over the next several decades, as white settlement continued to push westward, Indian removal and containment would resume. The concept of the "reservation" would come to dominate federal policy. And the old tribal worlds would shrink to scattered islands on a map drawn by strangers. ◆

This Land Is My Land

Imagine having someone tell you where you can or cannot live. The same attitudes that permitted the government to "remove" tribes from their homelands (whether by bullets or by treaties) have found many different expressions through the years.

Well into the 20th century, African Americans were openly forbidden or discouraged from owning property in certain neighborhoods. Some areas also systematically kept out Jews.

During World War II, Japanese Americans were evacuated from their homes and held in concentration camps, even though they were U.S. citizens. Even today, minorities often encounter illegal obstacles and open resistance when

ROUTES OF REMOVAL

- - - - - CHEROKEE
- - - - - CHOCTAW
- - - - - CHICKASAW
.... CREEK
.... SEMINOLE
———— Converging Routes

☐ Indian lands before relocation with dates of cession

THE INDIAN TERRITORY

Ft. Gibson
Ft. Coffee
Ft. Smith
Ft. Towson

1832
1830
1835
1832
Echota
Ft. Mitchell
1832

GULF OF MEXICO

they attempt to live in mostly white neighborhoods.

These infringements of freedom have sometimes been backed up by vandalism and personal violence. History teaches us that in order for people of different backgrounds or habits or beliefs to coexist peacefully, they first have to respect one another's right to exist at all.

In one way or another, we all prefer the familiar to the unknown. Familiar people, languages, environments and lifestyles help make our lives comfortable and our relationships with others predictable. When we feel that the differences between us outweigh the things we have in common, we sometimes react to each other with hostility and fear. Sometimes, in the back of our minds, we're afraid that what we don't know can hurt us.

Fear of the unknown has been a hidden cause of many human conflicts. From the earliest times, differences of skin color, language, customs and religion have made people suspicious of one another: What are those strangers talking about in their mysterious tongue? Differences challenge our natural assumptions about ourselves, about the "rightness" of the way we are. Often the easiest response is to assume that those who are different must be "wrong."

In 1492, Native Americans and Europeans seemed as different to each other as humans and space aliens would seem today. How would we want a crew of galactic explorers to treat us? How would we treat them?

(Continued from page 20)

Letter from a Choctaw Chief

up the stake and wiped out all traces of the line. I will not conceal from you my fears, that the present grounds may be removed. ... Who of us can tell after witnessing what has already been done, what the next force may be. I ask you in the name of justice, for repose for myself and for my injured people. Let us alone — we will not harm you, we want rest. ... As east of the Mississippi we have been friends, so west we will cherish the same feelings with additional fervour; and although we may be removed to the desert, still we shall look with fond regard, upon those who have promised us their protection. ...

Friends, my attachment to my native land was strong — that cord is now broken; and we must go forth as wanderers in a strange land! ... Let me intreat you to regard us with feelings of kindness, and when the hand of oppression is stretched against us, let me hope that a warning voice may be heard from every part of the U[nited] States, filling the mountains and valleys with echo, and say stop, you have no power, we are the sovereign people, and our red friends shall no more be disturbed.

No Promised Land

Like the Quakers, the early Mormons were feared and distrusted by their neighbors. When Mormons settled in Missouri in the 1830s, local residents found Mormon beliefs and practices not simply strange, but wrong. And the solution they sought was just as extreme as the banishment and death penalty laws against Massachusetts Quakers. The Mormons, the Missouri governor declared, must be removed — if not by expulsion, then by extermination.

SHORTLY AFTER HIS ARRIVAL in Jackson County, Mo., in 1831, the Mormon prophet Joseph Smith announced that he had discovered there the site of the Garden of Eden. But the life that Smith's followers (Latter-day Saints, as they called themselves) found in their new home was a far cry from Paradise.

The "frontier" state of Missouri had strong ties to the South, where most of its citizens originally came from. The Mormons, moving in from New England and Canada, brought a different way of life and point of view. Many of Missouri's pioneers saw the newcomers as religious fanatics greedy for land and political power. The Mormons' belief in a modern prophet and modern scripture (Smith's *Book of Mormon*) made their more traditional Protestant neighbors suspicious. Further, the Mormons pooled their resources and tended to vote as an organized block. To the old settlers, both of these practices seemed like a direct challenge to frontier individualism.

Since the Mormons opposed slavery, their

influence on elections threatened Missouri's status as a slave state. Rumors circulated that the Mormons planned to convert local slaves and Indians and enlist them in overthrowing the state government.

The tensions and ill will between Mormons and Missourians ran both ways. Mormon settlers established the first schools in northwest Missouri and sometimes looked down on their less cultivated neighbors as intellectually as well as morally inferior. They declared that they had a divine mission to establish God's kingdom among the heathen. Mormon preachers warned that God was preparing to punish the "enemies" of the Church.

The Missourians interpreted these teachings as an open threat. In 1833, some took up arms and began harassing Mormon leaders. They tarred and feathered Bishop Edward Partridge. They wrecked the Church's printing press and vandalized a Mormon store. Two Missourians and one Mormon died in skirmishes.

It wasn't long before all of the Latter-day Saints were driven out of Jackson County. Most of the refugees spent a brutal winter in makeshift camps and abandoned slave cabins along the Missouri River. Hunting and scavenging didn't provide enough food. The weakened population fell prey to one illness after another.

Joseph Smith recruited 200 Ohioans to help his people win their homes back, but he scrapped the plan when the Missouri governor refused to support it. The residents of neighboring Clay County offered the exiles a temporary refuge. Three years later, vigilante activity there made county leaders fear further violence, so they asked the Mormons to leave.

Several prominent Missourians felt that the Mormons had been treated unfairly. They proposed the creation of a separate county where the Latter-day Saints could settle without interference. The state legislature organized Caldwell County for this purpose in 1836, setting aside Daviess County, to the north, for displaced non-Mormons.

For a while segregation preserved the peace. Many residents of surrounding counties assumed that the Mormons would stay within their new boundaries. But when thousands of

Above. Mormons followed their leaders through the wilderness in search of a place to call home.

Below. Joseph Smith, the founder of Mormonism, believed that Missouri was the Promised Land for his people.

new Mormon arrivals overflowed Caldwell County in 1838, the old conflicts resumed.

Another development that strained relations between Latter-day Saints and Missourians occurred inside the Mormon community. Some Mormons believed that standing their ground would require better discipline and unity. In June 1838, hard-liners formed an organization called the Danites to monitor and regulate the conduct of the Saints. Within a few months, the group comprised nearly 400 men. To the Missourians who saw them marching and drilling, the Danites seemed less like an internal police force than like a standing army.

Throughout the summer, tensions continued to rise. As the Latter-day Saints sharpened their militant image, residents of the northwestern counties organized anti-Mormon campaigns. These ranged from public speeches and referendums to armed attacks. When a Daviess County politician proposed barring Mormons from voting in the August 6 election, a brawl erupted.

Both sides gave in to a growing spirit of lawlessness. Mormons and Missourians poached each other's livestock, burned each other's corncribs and shot into the windows of each other's homes. The pattern of rumor and raid and retaliation quickly became so widespread and familiar that no one could sort out how it all started. Both sides, in turn, asked Governor Lilburn Boggs to send in the state militia.

On October 23, a Methodist minister named Samuel Bogart decided not to wait for the governor's decision. As captain of the Ray County militia, he called out 35 men to patrol the Caldwell County line and head off a suspected Mormon invasion. Armed and impressively outfitted in white blanket coats and knife-belts, Bogart's troops surprised Mormons in their houses and made them surrender their weapons.

The following day, the militia captured two Mormon spies inside Ray County. Word shot through the Mormon territory that Bogart was threatening to execute his captives. At the same time, two dissident Mormons signed affidavits describing a secret army of Church members. From the statehouse to the humblest farmhouse, everyone waited for the tensions to explode.

A Mormon brigade set out to rescue the spies at Crooked River on October 25. A battle erupted, leaving three Mormons and one Missourian dead. Reports of the conflict convinced state military commanders to mobilize their troops to subdue a rumored Mormon uprising. More significantly, the rumors prompted Governor Boggs to act.

The military order from the governor's office was dated October 27, 1838. It stated, in part: "The Mormons must be

"The Mormons must be treated as enemies, and must be driven from the state."

A Survivor's Story

Mrs. Amanda Smith lost her husband and son in the Haun's Mill Massacre.

The next day the mob came back. They told us we must leave the State forthwith or be killed. It was bad weather, and they had taken our teams and clothes; our men were all dead or wounded. I told them they might kill me and my children, and welcome. They said to us, from time to time, if we did not leave the State they would come and kill us. We could not leave then. We had little prayer meetings; they said if we did not stop them they would kill every man, woman, and child. We had spelling schools for our little children; they pretended they were "Mormon meetings," and said if we did not stop them they would kill every man, woman, and child. ...

I started the 1st of February, very cold weather, for Illinois, with five small children and no money. It was mob all the way. I drove the team, and we slept out of doors. We suffered greatly from hunger, cold, and fatigue; and for what? For our religion. In this boasted land of liberty, 'Deny your faith or die,' was the cry.

treated as enemies, and must be exterminated or driven from the State if necessary for the public peace — their outrages are beyond all description."

More than likely, news of the Extermination Order did not reach the Missouri militia troops positioned outside the Mormon village of Haun's Mill, in eastern Caldwell County. The 12 or so village families, along with more than that number living out of covered wagons, had decided to ignore Joseph Smith's call for all Mormons to gather at the town of Far West, on the other side of the county. Instead, they organized their own small militia and braced themselves against the surrounding Missourians.

The state troops stopped Mormons as they passed through the area on their way west. They turned some families back and demanded that others surrender their guns. The people of Haun's Mill began planning what they would do in case of attack. After several days of the standoff, both sides signed a peace treaty in order to avoid another bloody engagement like Crooked River. The Mormons kept their guards on the lookout, but no one really expected further trouble for a while.

Late in the afternoon on October 30, three companies of mounted militiamen advanced through the trees to the edge of the Mormon settlement. It was a warm, Indian-summer day, and children were playing on the creekbank. The grown-ups went about their chores. In front of one cabin, Rial Ames and Hyrum Abbott sat in straight chairs, taking turns cutting each other's hair. The front ranks of the state troops began walking out of the woods. From a distance of about 100 yards, Mr. Ames and Mr. Abbott mistook them for Mormon reinforcements.

One of the Missouri officers fired a warning

shot into the air. A long silence followed. As the troops approached, their red kerchiefs and black "war-paint" told the people of Haun's Mill that the truce was over. The state militia advanced under the orders "Shoot at everything wearing breeches, and shoot to kill."

Two hundred troops from three counties took part in the attack. Mormon men, women and children, startled from their activities, dashed for cover amid the thunder of guns and hooves. Several residents, including the local militia commander, waved their hats in appeal for mercy, but there was none. The onslaught drove many villagers south across the mill dam and into the woods. One woman heard 20 musket balls hit the log she was hiding behind.

The blacksmith shop had always seemed like the sturdiest structure at Haun's Mill and the easiest to defend. Now 15 men and three boys barricaded themselves inside it, armed with squirrel rifles and shotguns. The boys lay on the floor, under the big bellows that the blacksmith used to pump air into the forge. The long horizontal gaps in the log walls might have been good places to position firearms if the Mormons had been quick enough. But bullets kept spraying in from the outside. As the boys heard the men fall, they couldn't tell which of them were their fathers. Finally, the Missourians closed in and jammed their gun barrels through the cracks.

With half his fighters either dead or

Opposite page.
Continued persecution would eventually drive the Latter-day Saints westward on a grueling migration to Utah.

Above. The order came from Gov. Boggs that all Mormons were to be expelled from Missouri or "exterminated."

Below. The surprise attack on Haun's Mill threw the village into chaos.

Righting Old Wrongs

By the time the first few Mormon families moved back into Jackson County in 1867, the old hostilities no longer threatened their freedom or safety. Nonetheless, Gov. Boggs' Extermination Order remained on the books until a subsequent governor proclaimed the following in 1976:

WHEREAS, on October 27, 1838, the Governor of the State of Missouri, Lilburn W. Boggs, issued an order calling for the extermination or expulsion of Mormons from the State of Missouri; and

WHEREAS, Governor Boggs' order clearly contravened the rights to life, liberty, property and religious freedom as guaranteed by the Constitution of the United States, as well as the Constitution of the State of Missouri; and

WHEREAS, in this Bicentennial year as we reflect on our nation's heritage, the exercise of religious freedom is without question one of the basic tenets of our free democratic republic;

NOW, THEREFORE, I, CHRISTOPHER S. BOND, Governor of the State of Missouri, by virtue of the authority vested in me by the Constitution and the laws of the State of Missouri, do hereby ... rescind Executive Order Number 44 dated October 27, 1838, issued by Governor Lilburn W. Boggs.

wounded, Mormon militia commander David Evans ordered the others to attempt an escape. For most, it amounted to a suicide run. An old man named Thomas McBride, who had fought under George Washington in the Revolutionary War, suffered a hit and handed over his rifle to the oncoming Missourians. One of these, ferry operator Jacob Rogers from Daviess County, aimed McBride's own weapon at him and shot him through the chest. Then Rogers bent over the old man's body and slashed it repeatedly with a corn-cutter.

Missouri troops entered the blacksmith shop, which was now eerily silent. Their boots tracked through a pool of blood. Under the bellows, the men found Sardius Smith, 10 years old and trembling.

Livingston County militiaman William Reynolds let him plead for mercy before shooting the top of the boy's head off, point-blank. "Nits will make lice," Reynolds was later quoted as saying, "and if he had lived he would have become a Mormon." Warren Smith, Sardius' father, was one of the few Mormon men in the room still barely alive.

In all, 18 residents of Haun's Mill died. Fifteen more were wounded. Three state troopers suffered injuries. Before the Missourians left the village, some of them ransacked empty houses and wagons and even corpses. A number of wounded Mormons had their clothes torn off while pretending to be dead.

The next morning, Amanda Smith

walked back out of the woods. Her village, which just the day before had enjoyed the prospect of peace, was now littered with bodies. Amanda said a prayer as she entered the blacksmith shop, sickened at the fear of what she would find there. Warren, her husband, and Sardius, her son, lay motionless and cold. When Amanda cried out, she saw movement in a heap of corpses. From under the pile emerged her other son, Alma. All night he had listened and waited.

No one knew whether the state militia would return. There wasn't time for proper burials, so the survivors dropped the bodies of their friends and loved ones down an old well. They added a layer of dirt and straw to keep away vultures.

News of the governor's Extermination Order traveled with the news of the massacre at Haun's Mill. Both sides were anxious now for the conflict to end. Over the winter, military courts and county courts and the state legislature considered the fate of the Mormons in Missouri.

Joseph Smith was among several Saints confined to prison on charges of riot and treason. By February 1839, at Smith's urging, his followers had begun their exodus from the state. On April 16, he escaped captivity and joined the new settlement in Illinois. Anti-Mormon sentiment there would result five years later in his murder by a mob. ◆

Opposite page.
Women and children who escaped the onslaught hid in the woods all night.

AT ISSUE

Whose Right?

A political candidate in Missouri proposed denying Mormons the vote in the 1838 election. When officials failed to take this action, some citizens of Daviess County verbally and physically attacked Mormons as they came to cast their ballots.

The right to vote, also called suffrage or the franchise, is such a basic element of our democracy that many Americans take it for granted: No one, we are sure, has the power to bar us from the polls. Yet history shows that this right has not been easily won.

During the colonial period, only white men who owned a certain amount of property were allowed to participate in the electoral process. After the Revolutionary War, the states began setting different standards. Pennsylvania, for example, extended voting rights to all free adult males who were taxpayers.

The movement for women's suffrage developed out of the abolitionist movement of the early 1800s, when many women took part in the public outcry against slavery. The State of Wyoming became the first to guarantee women the right to vote when it entered the Union in 1890. Over the next 30 years, other states followed, and the 19th Amendment enfranchised women nationwide in 1920.

African American men won full citizenship, including the right to vote, after slavery was abolished in 1865. In some areas, however, particularly the South, state and local governments set voting requirements that limited black participation. For example, the poll tax — a fee charged to all voters — was a greater burden on blacks because their incomes were lower than those of whites. Other requirements, such as reading tests, were applied unequally to the two races. Not until the Voting Rights Act of 1965 did African Americans gain equal access to the ballot.

The civil rights movement of the 1960s also brought Native Americans a stronger voice in government. Native Americans were granted citizenship in 1924, but measures similar to those used against Southern blacks had limited their participation in many areas.

During the Vietnam War, young Americans argued that if 18-year-olds were eligible for the draft, then they should also be allowed to vote. The 26th Amendment lowered the voting age from 21 to 18 in 1971.

By gradually opening the doors of the political process, the extension of the right to vote has reflected a changing conception of "us" and "them."

HARRIET JACOBS HAD SUCH A sheltered and carefree early childhood in Edenton, N.C., that she was 6 years old before she knew she was a slave. Harriet's father, Daniel, was a carpenter who supported himself like a free man, although he had to pay his owner $200 a year for the privilege. Her grandmother, Molly Horniblow, earned good money selling her famous pastries to the women of Edenton.

Because the Jacobses belonged to a city family, they enjoyed more freedom of move-

Harriet Jacobs Owns Herself

For their first 246 years on this continent, African Americans were treated as possessions, not people. Although the Declaration of Independence declared all men equal, the United States Constitution defined a slave as equivalent to three-fifths of a free man. Slaves could not vote, own property or, in most cases, earn money. They had no right to an education. Many were not allowed to marry the person of their choice. The slave market often separated wives from husbands and parents from children.

Yet, even under these conditions, the strongest of human aspirations survived. The story of Harriet Jacobs reminds us of the multitude whose names are forgotten.

ment than plantation slaves. It was not until 1819, when her mother died, that Harriet learned she was someone else's property.

Young Harriet knew her grandmother's stories about being freed as a child and captured back into slavery, about later seeing each of her five children sold to a different master. But Harriet's mistress taught her to read and write and sew and led her to believe that one day she would get her freedom. Then the mistress died. In her will, she left 11-year-old Harriet to a 3-year-old niece.

Harriet's young owner was the daughter of Dr. and Mrs. Norcom, who had also bought Harriet's younger brother, John, for their son. Slave life at the Norcoms' was the nightmare that Harriet

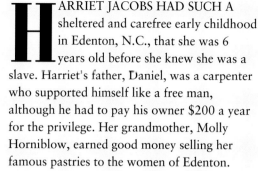

"In the Night Season"

The personal activities of slaves were severely regulated. The General Court of Connecticut Colony enacted a law that reveals the fear with which slave owners regarded their human property.

Be it enacted by the Governour, Council and Representatives, in General Court assembled, and by the authority of the same, That from and after the publication of this act, if any negro or Indian servant or slave shall be found abroad from home in the night season, after nine of the clock, without special order from his or their master or mistress, it shall be lawful for any person or persons to apprehend and secure such negro or Indian servant or slave so offending, and him or them bring before the next assistant or justice of peace; which ... shall have full power to ... order him or them to be publickly whipt on his or their naked body, not exceeding ten stripes, and pay cost of court, except his or their master or mistress shall redeem them by paying a fine not exceeding twenty shillings.

had only heard tales about until now. The first time Harriet wore some new winter shoes her grandmother had given her, Mrs. Norcom asked what was making such a horrible squeak.

"Take them off," she said, "and if you put them on again, I'll throw them into the fire." After Harriet removed the shoes, Mrs. Norcom sent her on a long errand in the snow. That night Harriet's throat was so sore that she thought she might die. In the morning, she was almost disappointed to find herself well again.

Harriet and John's father died later that year. While his wake was taking place less than a mile away, Mrs. Norcom made Harriet stay and decorate the Norcom house for a party.

Grandmother Molly grieved to see the children mistreated. She saved every penny she could in the hope of some day being able to purchase her entire family. In the meantime, whenever Harriet passed by her grandmother's place, Molly secretly handed her a treat — Mrs. Norcom didn't allow the girl to stop for visits.

Molly's mistress — Mrs. Norcom's mother — had always promised to free Molly in her will. But when the old lady died, Dr. Norcom decided that Molly had to be sold instead. Molly's many white friends in Edenton were horrified when she stepped up, straight and calm, onto the auction block. For a long time, no one offered a bid. Then a woman called out, "Fifty dollars." It was the dead mistress's maiden sister, who knew Molly well. The sister couldn't read or write, but she marked an 'X' on the bill of sale and then gave Molly her freedom.

Dr. Norcom frequently received high offers for Harriet, but he turned them all down. In public, he said that she wasn't his, but his daughter's. In private, however, he followed a different policy. When Harriet was 15, the 50-year-old Dr. Norcom raped her. The attacks continued, and Norcom swore he would kill her if she didn't remain "silent as the grave."

Harriet knew of at least 11 slave children that Dr. Norcom had fathered. She

had seen him sell them and their mothers away. But Dr. Norcom refused to let Harriet go. When she fell in love with a young freeborn carpenter in the neighborhood, Norcom ordered her never again to speak the man's name. He said that if the suitor came back to see her he would "shoot him as soon as I would a dog." Reluctantly, Harriet broke off the relationship.

Dr. Norcom's behavior was no secret to his neighbors. Samuel Sawyer, a prominent citizen and a bachelor, took an interest in Harriet's plight, and the two soon developed a mutual affection. Harriet knew that her relationship with a white man of her own choosing would enrage Norcom. In fact, she hoped it would. She was now more determined than ever to repel her master's advances.

Norcom did become furious, but he rejected Sawyer's offer to buy Harriet. When Harriet's affair with Sawyer produced a son, the doctor reminded the new mother that any child of hers belonged to him. Harriet gave birth at her grandmother's and stayed on there with her baby, Joseph. Norcom's wife threatened to kill Harriet if Norcom brought her back to their home.

Molly's house was like a peaceful island in a troubled sea. Her pastry business supported the family in modest comfort. Here Harriet watched little Joseph grow and prayed for his freedom. Yet, across the South, conditions were worsening for slaves. In 1830, North Carolina made it a crime, punishable by 39 lashes, to teach a slave how to read. The next year, slaves were forbidden to gather for prayer meetings. Slave owners were so fearful of an uprising that they even attempted to deny slaves the refuge of religion.

In late August 1831, the slave owners' worst fear came true. Forty miles north of Edenton, in Southampton County, Va., a slave preacher named Nat Turner led a revolt that left 55 white people dead. The incident sent a wave of terror over the whole region.

In Edenton, angry whites shouldered their rifles and marched through town. Among these were many who were too poor to own slaves but who enjoyed having a "lower" group to look down on and took special pleasure in this opportunity to harass blacks. Many slave women and children hid in the woods and swamps while their cabins were searched and ransacked. Any suspicious document or trace of ammunition — including items planted by the searchers — could be considered proof of a "plot."

The ruffians searching Harriet's grandmother's house found a trunk packed with fine linens that she had bought and cared for over the years. When the men asked Molly where a "nigger" stole such things, she said certainly not from any of their houses. One fellow hooted and waved some papers he'd found. The leader of the group took the sheaf and began reading out loud — fancy poetry! The disappointed hoodlums raided Molly's jelly cupboard for a taste from each jar before going out to trample her garden.

Nat Turner eluded his pursuers for more than two months. Following his widely

> *Slave owners were so fearful of an uprising that they even attempted to deny slaves the refuge of religion.*

Left. A traveler from Canada sketched this scene at a Charleston, S.C., slave auction.

the test. He seemed to them to be the Devil on Earth. When he learned that Harriet was expecting another child by Mr. Sawyer, he came and chopped off all her hair with rough shears. The birth of a daughter made Harriet grieve — she knew that slavery was even harder for women than it was for men.

While the little girl, Louisa, was still a baby, Harriet arranged to have her and Joseph baptized. The former owner of Harriet's father invited the family to her house after the ceremony. The old woman brought out a tiny gold chain and fastened it around Louisa's neck. Harriet expressed her gratitude but said that she could abide no chain on her daughter, not even one of pure gold.

More than anything, Harriet longed to escape with her children from bondage. One day Dr. Norcom proposed a single condition for their freedom — that Harriet cease all contact with Sawyer. She didn't believe him for a minute. She knew it was another trick. If any white man was going to help her, it was Sawyer. When she refused Norcom's offer, he ordered the three of them sent to his son's plantation, six miles outside of town.

Six-year-old Joseph was sick on the appointed day, so Harriet and Louisa left him at Molly's. Young Norcom put Harriet to work immediately, preparing the house for his new bride. Louisa, age 3, spent her long, solitary days crying. One morning she crawled up under the big house and cried herself sick. As Harriet was pulling her out, young Norcom appeared, frowning, and then walked away. The next day, he let Harriet send Louisa back to town in a cart loaded with shingles.

All alone now, Harriet missed the smiles of her children, the strength and consolation of her grandmother. She had to get used to the roughness of plantation life. One Monday evening she watched as the foremen of the field hands passed out weekly rations of smoked meat, herring and corn. An old slave who had served three generations of Norcoms waited in the line. Harriet heard the mistress — Norcom's new wife — tell the foreman the man didn't deserve a ration. She said that when a slave got too old to work, he "ought to be fed on grass."

Harriet went about her assigned duties but kept her mind on one thing: escape. After her master offered to let her move from the

publicized capture, torture, trial and execution, white outrage subsided somewhat, although daily patrols continued in some districts. It now occurred to local planters that a little religion among the slaves might not be such a bad idea — it might, in fact, keep them from murdering their owners! Local churches began holding special slave services. "If you disobey your earthly master," white preachers warned, "you offend your Heavenly Master."

Molly and Harriet believed that good would eventually overcome the evil of slavery. But Dr. Norcom once again put their faith to cramped slave quarters into the big house, she found her opportunity. One dark rainy midnight she jumped out a window and ran off the plantation unobserved.

She stopped by Molly's without waking her and looked in on the children. She stayed a few nights at a friend's house, then fled from a search party and spent a week in a thicket. A snakebite forced her back into town, where an old woman saved her life by drawing the poison out with copper pennies steeped in vinegar. A slave-owning woman friend of Molly's offered a place to hide — under a floorboard in her kitchen. The woman's cook helped Harriet into the hole and covered her with a quilt. Then she laid a buffalo skin over the plank. All day long, the cook "talked to herself" to keep the runaway from getting lonely.

Dr. Norcom first offered a $100 reward for Harriet's capture. Then he placed her young children, along with her brother John and her Aunt Betty, in jail at his own expense to force them to reveal her hiding place. They remained silent. Six-year-old Joe made a new mark on his cell door every day.

The talk around Edenton was that Harriet had fled to New York. Dr. Norcom believed this and went looking for her. Sawyer reasoned that the cost of such a trip, along with that of holding the prisoners, might make the doctor willing to consider a sale. Sawyer arranged to buy John, Joe and Louisa. The day they got out, Joe counted 60 marks on the door.

Harriet rejoiced to hear the news. She knew that very soon Sawyer would free the children as he had promised. Her friends and loved ones now set Harriet on a new plan. They decided it wasn't safe for her to remain where she was. The cook brought her a sailor suit and a small bundle of supplies.

"Put your hands in your pockets," the cook said, "and walk rickety, like the sailors." This wasn't hard to do, after weeks of lying under a cold floor!

The plan was for Harriet to hide out on a boat on Albemarle Sound while Uncle Joe made other arrangements. When the boat became too risky, her uncle's friend

Peter hacked out a den for her in a bamboo swamp. There were snakes all around, and the tobacco that Peter burned to keep away mosquitoes gave Harriet a headache. She was grateful that the snakes, at least, refrained from biting.

It thrilled Harriet to learn that the place Uncle Joe had prepared for her was back at her grandmother's. Mr. Sawyer had sent the children to live there. She couldn't wait to see them again. She knew there was danger involved — as there was in everything she did now — but she never imagined the difficulties.

Her new dwelling was a cramped attic above a storage shed on Molly's patio. It had no windows or air vents— only a trapdoor. The total darkness meant that rats and mice crawled around her constantly. Roaches and spiders were her other companions. Molly or Uncle Joe or Aunt Betty slipped food and whispered encouragement through the trapdoor at night, but it wasn't safe to tell the children where she was. Harriet could only listen when they played nearby. One day she found a small drill that Uncle Joe had forgotten and made a peephole that let her catch glimpses of them.

Gradually, Harriet's eyes grew accustomed to the dark. She even managed to read and sew. Time seemed as tedious and burdensome as her own movements — the ceiling was so low that, for exercise, all she could do was crawl. No one knew how long she would have to stay there. Season gave way to season. At first, the heat of late summer made sap drip from the roof shingles. Autumn was mild, but the winter chill cut like a knife.

For Christmas, she made Joe and Louisa each a new outfit with material that Molly brought her. On Christmas morning, she overheard some of the other children saying that Santa Claus was really their own mothers. Joe told them that this was impossible: His mother was up north in New York, but his stocking had been filled.

To Harriet's outrage, Dr. Norcom continued to badger Molly. He bluffed that he knew where the escapee was and would soon have her. With the help of Uncle Joe and his friend Peter, Harriet arranged to have some letters sent to New York to be

FIRST PERSON

A Slave Auction

Solomon Northup, born in 1808 to free black parents in Minerva, N.Y., was kidnapped into slavery while on a visit to Washington at the age of 33. He endured 12 years of bondage in Louisiana before New York State officials, along with Solomon's wife, helped win his freedom. He published a memoir of this period, Twelve Years A Slave, *in 1853. The following excerpt describes a New Orleans slave auction:*

Mr. Theophilus Freeman bustled about in a very industrious manner, getting his property ready for the sales-room, intending, no doubt, to do that day a rousing business.

In the first place we were required to wash thoroughly, and those with beards, to shave. We were then furnished with a new suit each, cheap, but clean. The men had hat, coat, shirt, pants and shoes; the women frocks of calico, and handkerchiefs to bind about their heads. ...

The men were arranged on one side of the room, the women on the other. The tallest was placed at the head of the row, then the next tallest, and so on in the order of their respective heights. ...

He would make us hold up our heads, walk briskly back and forth, while customers would

(Continued on page 36)

(Continued from page 35)

A Slave Auction

feel of our hands and arms and bodies, turn us about, ask us what we could do, make us open our mouths and show our teeth, precisely as a jockey examines a horse which he is about to barter for or purchase.

During the day ... a number of sales were made. ... Lethe was sold to a planter of Baton Rouge, her eyes flashing with anger as she was led away.

The same man also purchased Randall. The little fellow was made to jump, and run across the floor, and perform many other feats, exhibiting his activity and condition. All the time the trade was going on, Eliza was crying aloud, and wringing her hands. She besought the man not to buy [her son], unless he also bought herself and Emily [her daughter]. She promised, in that case, to be the most faithful slave that ever lived.

The man answered that he could not afford it, and then Eliza burst into ... grief, weeping plaintively. Freeman turned round to her, savagely, with his whip in his uplifted hand, ordering her to stop her noise, or he would flog her. He would not have such work — such snivelling; and unless she ceased that minute, he would take her to the yard and give her a hundred lashes.

mailed back to Edenton. In them, she wrote to Dr. Norcom and to Molly that she was moving on to Boston, where the Abolitionist movement was strong. Dr. Norcom believed what he read.

Despite numerous promises, Sawyer still had not freed the children. He decided that Louisa should be sent to live in Brooklyn with his cousin, who had a little girl. Harriet feared that her daughter was being sent as a servant, but she was powerless to halt the plan. Even Mrs. Norcom objected, on the grounds that her daughter had never signed Louisa's bill of sale. According to Aunt Betty, the Norcoms' cook, Mrs. Norcom said that when Louisa left it was as if Mr. Sawyer had walked into her parlor and stolen a piece of furniture.

Aunt Betty was Harriet's main link to the outside world. And it was Aunt Betty, more than anyone, who urged Harriet to take her chance at freedom. On the first day of January 1842 — the seventh New Year's that Harriet had passed in the attic — Aunt Betty came with some news. That morning their neighbor Fanny had been sold at the annual New Year's auction. As her purchasers were taking her to her new home, Fanny escaped. Harriet felt the same excitement Aunt Betty did. They prayed that Fanny would make it and that Harriet's turn would be next.

A few days later, little Joe reported to Molly that he had caught sight of Fanny in her mother's house, right next door. Molly made him promise not to tell anyone else, but she did tell Harriet. It made Harriet both sad and hopeful to think of another fugitive so close by.

Aunt Betty took ill and died later that year, before Harriet could make their dream come true. Mrs. Norcom told the preacher that she wanted her faithful cook buried in the Norcom family cemetery. Molly, who was Betty's mother, thanked Mrs. Norcom just the same but had the grave dug in the slave burial grounds. Uncle Joe paid for an elaborate funeral for his sister, though Molly knew that most of Edenton assumed the Norcoms had done it all.

With Aunt Betty gone, Harriet had no one to talk with about her schemes. But she

Left. For field slaves who often labored into the night, it was a relief to stop work at sundown.

was determined to find a way north. Uncle Joe's friend Peter knocked on the trapdoor one night to tell her he'd found a captain who would take her. Molly cried when she heard it, knowing there was no changing the girl's mind.

On the day Harriet was to leave, Peter informed her that the ship had been delayed. Harriet had spent seven years in the attic, but now she wasn't sure she could stand it for one more minute. Then word came that another fugitive slave had been brutally murdered. Molly talked Harriet out of going at such a treacherous time. A spell of bad weather kept the ship in harbor.

> *They knew all too well the world they were leaving. They could only dream of the one that lay ahead.*

Molly feared that the whole plan had fallen apart now, that they would all be found out. One morning she helped Harriet climb down to discuss the matter and forgot to lock the storeroom door. A housemaid called for Molly from the patio and barged in just as Harriet was darting behind some barrels. The maid said nothing, but Molly felt certain the secret was out. She had no choice now but to give Harriet her blessing, along with some travel money.

Molly brought little Joe, 12 years old now, to see his mother. He wasn't even surprised. Several years before, he said, he had heard her cough overhead. He figured out that she was hiding there and that if he told anyone about it she might die. Harriet told him that as soon as she got her own freedom, she'd start working for his.

Peter led Harriet to the small boat that would take her to the big one. The captain welcomed her and showed her to her tiny room. There sat Fanny, who thought she must be seeing a ghost. The two friends hugged for a long time and cried. They knew all too well the world they were leaving. They could only dream of the one that lay ahead. They listened to the great timbered hull cutting the water — nothing but water between them and Philadelphia.

When she arrived in the North, Harriet

Closed Doors

Before the Emancipation Proclamation, many of the states in which slavery was illegal nonetheless placed harsh restrictions on African Americans. According to the 1851 constitution of Indiana, only "white male citizens" were allowed to vote. Further, the document specified, "No negro or mulatto shall have the right of suffrage." Other provisions defined the status of blacks more fully.

ART. XII., SEC. 1. The militia shall consist of all able-bodied white male persons. ...

ART. XIII., SEC. 1. No negro or mulatto shall come into, or settle in the State after the adoption of this Constitution.

SEC. 2. All contracts made with any negro or mulatto coming into the State contrary to the foregoing section shall be void; and any person who shall employ such negro or mulatto or encourage him to remain in the State shall be fined not less than ten, nor more than five hundred dollars.

realized her adventures had just begun. Her first task was to reunite her family. She learned that Mr. Sawyer had transferred ownership of Joe and Louisa to Molly, who was a free woman. Harriet instructed Molly to send Joe north and then brought Louisa there herself.

Three times Harriet eluded capture by slavecatchers before a woman she worked for arranged to buy her and officially set her free. Encouraged by her brother John, who was gaining a reputation as a lecturer in abolitionist circles, Harriet offered her talents to the organized antislavery movement.

Her new friends urged her to write and

Harriet Jacobs

publish the story of her experiences in bondage. In 1861, a Boston firm issued the first printing of *Incidents in the Life of a Slave Girl,* Harriet Jacobs' autobiography. The book was published in England the following year. During and after the Civil War, Harriet worked in the Quaker relief effort in Virginia and Georgia, distributing clothes and seeds, teaching, and caring for the sick and wounded. For a time, she operated a boardinghouse in Cambridge, Mass. In 1896, Harriet's daughter, Louisa Matilda, was one of the organizers of the National Association of Colored Women.

Harriet Jacobs died on March 7, 1897, in Washington, D.C. She is buried near her brother John in Mount Auburn Cemetery, Cambridge. ◆

Jim Crow Is Watching

At the end of the Civil War, the 13th Constitutional Amendment outlawed slavery. In the next few years, the 14th and 15th amendments guaranteed African Americans the full rights of citizenship. The decade of Reconstruction brought blacks into public life and public office across the South. Still, even a bloody defeat on the battlefield and the long arm of Congress couldn't loosen the grip of white power for very long.

By 1877, corrupt politicians and racist organizations like the Ku Klux Klan had begun to intimidate blacks into surrendering their hard-won equality. Lynch mobs carried out a bloody campaign of vigilante justice *(see p. 108).* Whites regained their former domination of local and state governments. They began passing laws that openly favored whites and redefined blacks as second-class citizens. The segregation laws acquired the name "Jim Crow" from a popular blackface minstrel song.

A rigid barrier between the races was enforced by separate schools, restrooms, waiting rooms, drinking fountains and seating areas in movie theaters and on trains and buses. Commercial facilities such as restaurants and laundromats could refuse service to blacks altogether. In addition, poll taxes and other measures limited black participation in elections. By denying African Americans educational, economic and political opportunities, these laws instituted a social system that was closer to slavery than to true freedom.

The Jim Crow system survived a serious legal challenge in 1896. In the case of *Plessy v. Ferguson,* the U.S. Supreme Court approved the use of separate facilities as long as they were equal. In practice, of course, the facilities were rarely equal. It would take another 60 years, however, for the courts to declare separate facilities inherently unequal. Anti-lynching campaigns and other national movements in the early 1900s focused national attention on injustices in the South. But not until the civil rights movement of the late 1950s was the Jim Crow system dismantled and replaced with fair and impartial laws.

The following are some examples of Jim Crow laws and provisions:

• That if any Negro, mulatto, or other person of color shall intrude himself into ... any railroad car or other public vehicle set apart for the exclusive accommodation of white people, he shall be deemed guilty of a misdemeanor and, upon conviction, shall be sentenced to stand in pillory for one hour, or be whipped, not exceeding thirty-nine stripes, or both, at the discretion of the jury. (Florida, 1865)

• No property in a white section should ever be sold, rented, advertised, or offered to colored people. (Code of Ethics, Real Estate Board of Washington, D.C., 1948)

• It shall be unlawful for any person, firm, or corporation engaged in the business of cotton textile manufacturing in this state to allow or permit operatives, help and labor of the different races to labor and work together within the same room, or to use the same doors of entrance and exit at the same time, ... or to use the same stairway and windows at the same time, or to use at any time the same lavatories, toilets, drinking-water buckets, pails, cups, dippers, or glasses. (South Carolina, 1950s)

• It shall be unlawful for white and colored persons to play together ... in any game of cards, dice, dominoes, checkers, pool, billiards, softball, basketball, football, golf, track, and at swimming pools or in any athletic contest. (Montgomery, Ala., 1958)

Left. In the Jim Crow era, every sphere of activity was divided along racial lines.

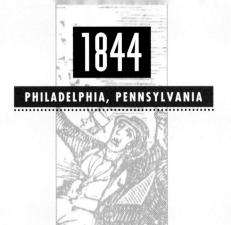

IN PENNSYLVANIA PUBLIC SCHOOLS in the 1840s, daily lessons from the King James Bible were required by law. In the opinion of Philadelphia's Protestant majority, this practice provided the moral underpinning of education.

To the city's growing minority of Irish Catholics, however, the "Bible law" represented forced indoctrination into the Protestant faith. The Catholic Church recognized a different version of the Christian scriptures, known as the Douai-Reims Bible,

In the City of Brotherly Love

The Irish and the English share a long legacy of conflict. Just before the English colonized America, they invaded Ireland and attempted to subdue its population of Catholic "savages." Many Irish families were even forced onto reservations to make room for English settlers.

When a wave of Irish Catholic immigrants began arriving in the U.S. in the 1820s, they found a bitter welcome among the Anglo-Saxon Protestant majority. Newspapers described them as "Irish niggers" and "a mongrel mass of ignorance." Many employers assigned Irish laborers to only the most menial and dangerous positions. Irish Catholicism was denounced with charges of superstition and perversion. In some cities, such as Philadelphia, anti-Catholic and anti-Irish hatred erupted into violence. Equally divisive as religious and ethnic differences, however, was the matter of immigration itself. In just half a century, native-born Americans had come to regard all new-comers as "them."

but Philadelphia authorities prohibited its use in the schools.

The mostly poor, working-class Irish immigrants of suburbs like Kensington and Southwark didn't yet have much of a voice in Philadelphia politics. But the resolution of a similar controversy in New York City inspired Philadelphia's Catholic bishop to petition the school board. Daily Bible reading was fine, Bishop Francis Kenrick wrote in November 1842, so long as Catholic students were allowed to use their own Bibles and were excused from Protestant devotional lessons. In January 1843, school officials granted the request.

The board's action didn't attract much notice at first. Eventually, however, a teacher lodged a complaint that the divided devotional was disrupting her classroom. When a Catholic board member and city alderman

Vicious, Ignorant and Foreign

Best known as the inventor of the telegraph, Samuel F. B. Morse (1791-1872) was an outspoken nativist who campaigned for restrictions on immigration. The following is an excerpt from a letter he wrote to the chairman of the Native American Democratic Association in 1836:

The question is now placed ... before the whole American people, whether it is or is not expedient that the naturalization laws be so altered as to put a stop to evils under which our democratic institutions are suffering, and to guard against dangers with which they are threatened from the influx of a vicious, ignorant foreign population; dangers enhanced by the combinations of these foreigners throughout the country; dangers still further enhanced by the present political movements of the civilized world, and the open as well as secret operations in the United States of Foreign Associations in Europe, and affiliated associations of foreigners throughout the country.

from Kensington named Hugh Clark advised the teacher to suspend all religious instruction until a better compromise could be reached, the issue threw Philadelphians into a face-off.

There was more at stake on both sides of this conflict than a simple choice of Bibles. For the city's largely native-born Protestants, control of school curriculum was just one of many privileges enjoyed by the majority. As descendants of early settlers in this cradle of the republic, they believed that the rising tide of immigrants threatened the long-standing political, economic, social and religious institutions of "native Americans."

The Irish Catholics, on the other hand, felt that they were entitled to a voice in their children's education and other areas of public life. Most of them had fled to the United States after Ireland's potato crops began to fail in the early 1800s. The emerging factory system

in the Northeast allowed them to begin new lives, if only on the lowest rung of the economic ladder.

This same system was taking jobs away from the skilled artisan class, to which most native Anglo-Saxon Protestants belonged. As a result, the ancient hatred between the English and the Irish quickly took root in American soil. Religious differences provoked open confrontation. In Philadelphia, as in Boston, New York and most other large cities, anti-Catholic and "nativist" organizations opposed the integration of new immigrants into U.S. society.

One such organization was the American Republicans, a Protestant political party in Philadelphia that became heavily involved in the school Bible controversy. The party held a rally to demand the resignation of alderman Hugh Clark from the school board. Nativist leaders sponsored a referendum in the 1844 spring election asking the public whether Catholic students should be permitted to read from the Catholic Bible.

Various groups used the campaign as an opportunity to denounce Catholicism as an evil foreign influence. Newspapers alleged that the Pope in Rome was pursuing a secret plan to seize control of American schools. Political candidates joined the local press in opposing the naturalization of foreigners as U.S. citizens. Protestant voters soundly rejected the two-Bible policy.

Alderman Hugh Clark introduced before the city legislature a resolution to ban Bible reading in the public schools. Again, the nativists united to defend the old state law. Their victory so angered Clark that he walked into Kensington School one morning during devotional, grabbed the Protestant Bible from the teacher's hands and proceeded to tear it page from page.

Events began to spiral out of control. As soon as word of Clark's defiance reached nativist leaders, they scheduled a protest meeting in the heart of Kensington. Residents of the district warned that such a gathering would bring trouble. As the outdoor rally assembled on Friday evening, May 3, 1844, Irish Catholics darted in and destroyed the speakers' platform. Onlookers began throwing bricks and rocks to disperse the crowd.

Philadelphia during this era lacked a police force capable of handling a large public disturbance. Only the sheriff of Philadelphia County had jurisdiction over the entire city, and his force was too small to concentrate in one troubled district. In the absence of effective law enforcement agencies, the nativists announced their plan to return to Kensington the following Monday.

Several thousand people heeded the call. In the middle of one of the opening speeches, an unexpected downpour swept over the area, scattering the multitude through the streets to find shelter. Most found their way to Nanny Goat Market, a pavilion large enough to accommodate the meeting.

Just as the speaker resumed addressing his rainsoaked and restless audience, someone fired a gun. A number of witnesses blamed a sniper from the nearby station house of the Hibernia Hose Company, an Irish fire brigade; others claimed that an argument within the crowd had sparked the shooting. Either way, one of the nativist protesters, an 18-year-old named George Schiffler, lay gravely wounded.

The assembly erupted in pandemonium.

Nativists by the hundreds stormed through the neighborhood, dislodging cobblestones to hurl through the windows of Irish stores and homes. Four men carried George Schiffler to an apothecary shop, where he died within an hour. Back at Nanny Goat Market, a band of Kensington residents attacked the remaining protesters with brickbats and pistols. One old Irishman in a sealskin cap took potshots with a musket.

The Irish and nativist factions regrouped on opposite sides of the market, skirmishing periodically throughout the evening. Philadelphia County Sheriff Morton McMichael arrived with several of his marshals during a lull around 7 p.m. and saw no need to exercise his authority.

By 10 o'clock, however, the nativists had swelled their ranks and were surging down Second Street toward the Female Roman Catholic Seminary. Faced with a rampage, Sheriff McMichael ordered his men to fire their rifles over the heads of the crowd. An assault on the seminary was averted, but angry nativists roamed the streets past midnight.

The next morning — Tuesday, May 7 — Philadelphians awoke to an uneasy calm. The *Native American* newspaper appeared with its front page banded in black for mourning. The guns were quiet, but on streetcorners around the city the usual commerce was punctuated by spontaneous anti-Catholic harangues. Bishop Kenrick issued a formal statement condemning Catholic participation in the turmoil and had copies posted in all districts. Within hours the nativists had removed these notices and folded them into paper hats.

Nativist leader Thomas Newbold announced a meeting to be held downtown that afternoon at 3 o'clock in Independence Square, a location that still symbolizes Philadelphia's role in the American Revolution. There the protesters passed voice-vote resolutions asserting their right to gather peaceably and charging the Catholics with attempting to drive the Bible out of the schools. Despite the pleadings of several leaders, the group elected

Anti-Catholic and "nativist" organizations opposed the integration of new immigrants into U.S. society.

Opposite page.

In 1834, nativists in Charlestown, Mass., burned Mount Benedict Convent.

to march once again into Kensington.

The Irish neighborhood was located about a mile and a half north of Independence Square. Along the way, the marchers shouted nativist slogans and waved a tattered American flag that they said had been trampled by Irishmen. With minimal warning, Kensington residents prepared to defend their homes and them-

Above. At times during the Philadelphia riots, the nativist mob overwhelmed the state militia.

selves. A distant roar and the shattering of windows announced the approaching mob.

No sooner had the market area begun to fill with nativists than a shot rang out from a house across the street, instantly killing one marcher. The crowd's attempt to charge the house was halted by a volley of gunfire from rooftops and windows. In sporadic confrontations over the next hour, three more marchers died. Still refusing to disband and flee, the nativists sent a small party to torch a building in which several snipers were hiding. The fire quickly consumed that structure and spread along the block. Within minutes, nearly 30 buildings were in flames, including Nanny Goat

Market. As soon as the Hibernia and Carroll fire brigades arrived on the scene, the rioters attacked them. Two engines and four carriages were destroyed.

Brig. Gen. Thomas Cadwalader, commander of the Pennsylvania militia, had had his men on alert since the day before. At 9 p.m. on Tuesday, at the height of the market fire, Sheriff McMichael called for Cadwalader to station his

Nativism and the Know-Nothings

All Americans — even those known today as Native Americans — are either descended from immigrants or are immigrants themselves. The first wave of immigration occurred more than 15,000 years ago, when people began entering the uninhabited continent on foot from northeastern Asia. Several thousand years later came explorers and missionaries and colonists from Europe. The slave trade of the 17th, 18th and 19th centuries brought a massive forced "immigration" of Africans.

The immigrants who organized the 13 American colonies were mostly English. For the first several decades after independence, the great majority of U.S. citizens shared an Anglo-Saxon Protestant heritage.

Beginning in the 1830s, economic and political turmoil in Europe sent people of many different ethnic groups to the United States. Germans, for example, settled across the Midwest, while Irish immigrants formed large communities in the Eastern cities. In most places, the new arrivals received a cold welcome: Native-born residents whose families had lived here for several generations suddenly felt overrun by strangers. Competition for jobs only heightened resentment toward immigrants.

Unfamiliar languages and accents were the most obvious "foreign" traits. More disturbing to many people were differences of religion. Many of the newcomers were Catholic, and mutual suspicions between Catholics and troops on the outskirts of Kensington. Around midnight, the order came to occupy the ravaged district. The soldiers succeeded in intimidating the mob without further violence by setting up loaded cannons in the streets. Under military escort, the fire companies hosed down the smoldering ruins.

By Wednesday morning, only three men — all Irish — had been arrested for their role in the disturbance. Following his arraignment for murder, John Taggert was escorted by several deputies to Northern Liberties Jail, thought to be a safe distance from Kensington. Along the way, a band of nativists seized Taggert, brutally beat him and got his neck in a noose before the deputies returned with enough help to save him.

Early in the afternoon, nativists began

Protestants in Europe dated back centuries.

Anti-foreigner prejudice stirred a variety of fears. Health risks were a well-publicized concern, especially in the crowded cities. New Yorkers wrongly blamed the Irish for an 1832 cholera epidemic. Protestant clergymen preached the dangers of Irish whiskey and German beer. The formation of ethnic social clubs and other organizations foreshadowed a new voice in American politics.

A growing sense of "us" and "them" gave rise to a movement called nativism. In 1849, a group of native-born Protestants in New York City formed the Order of the Star-Spangled Banner. Within a few years, secret nativist societies had been established in every major city. These groups published anti-immigrant and anti-Catholic literature and supported local political candidates who shared their views. From their policy of refusing to answer outsiders' questions about their organizations, members acquired the name Know-Nothings.

As nativist ideas became more popular in the 1850s, the movement emerged from secrecy and entered the national political arena. In 1855, forty-three members of Congress belonged to the Know-Nothing Party. But this prominence was short-lived. By the very next year, the issue of slavery — which divided the nation — had split the Know-Nothings and brought an end to organized nativism on a national scale.

Anti-immigration and anti-Catholic bigotry has periodically resurfaced. In the 1870s, recent European immigrants joined nativists in opposing Chinese immigration. Around the turn of the century, controversy arose over the large-scale immigration of Jews, Italians, Poles and other ethnic groups.

A similar influx of Asians and Latinos today has revived discussion about closing America's borders. Some cities in Florida and the southern border states have enacted ordinances mandating the use of "English language only" in public education. For a time in the 1980s, some Americans blamed Haitian immigrants for the spread of AIDS.

During his 1960 presidential campaign, John F. Kennedy faced questions about his loyalties because he was Catholic. In a speech to a group of Texas ministers, Kennedy explained how dividing the country into "us" and "them" endangers everyone: "For a while this year it may be a Catholic against whom the finger of suspicion is pointed. In other years it has been and may some day be again a Jew or a Quaker or a Unitarian or a Baptist. ... Today I may be the victim, but tomorrow it may be you."

Above. Nativist cartoons depicted the "dangers" of immigration.

Forging Hate

Prejudice leads some people to tell vicious lies about the groups they hate. And it can lead many others to believe them. In 1912, an anonymous Catholic-hater composed the following oath and claimed that it was sworn by all members of a Catholic fraternal organization.

I will, when opportunity presents, make and wage relentless war, secretly and openly, against all heretics, Protestants, and Masons, as I am directed to do, to extirpate them from the face of the whole earth; and that I will spare neither age nor sex, or condition, and that I will hang, burn, waste, boil, flay, strangle, and bury alive these infamous heretics, rip up the stomachs and wombs of their women, and crush their infants' heads against the wall in order to annihilate their execrable race. That when the same cannot be done openly, I will secretly use the poisonous cup, the strangulation cord, the steel of the [dagger], or the leaden bullet, regardless of the honor, rank, dignity, or authority of the persons, whatever may be their condition in life, either public or private, as I at any time may be directed to do so by any agents of the Pope or superior of the Brotherhood of the Holy Father of the Society of Jesus.

making their way back toward Kensington. The smell of smoke still hung in the air. Here and there, speakers railed against the Pope and demanded vengeance for the deaths of their comrades. Anticipating a replay of the night before, Irish Protestant and nativist residents of the district hung American flags and signs reading "Native American" in their windows. Some simply tacked up copies of the newspaper by that name. Each display drew a cheer from the passing throng.

Militia units patroling the area were unable to quell the unrest. As momentum gathered, marchers forcibly entered Irish homes to search for weapons. New fires, deliberately set, destroyed or damaged several more blocks by late afternoon. Emboldened by these exploits, the nativists broadened their aim and struck out toward downtown Philadelphia.

Mayor John Morin Scott, summoned from his daughter's birthday party, met the mob as it reached St. Augustine's Roman Catholic Church, at the corner of Fourth and Vine. The mayor spoke from the church steps, calling for reason and calm and denying a rumor that the building contained stored weapons. With this he explained that he himself was carrying the key.

Suddenly, a hurled stone hit the mayor in the chest, knocking the breath out of him. Police guards hurriedly bundled him away. The rioters, now confident that the church was undefended, lifted two boys over the fence to begin the destruction. The youngsters broke in through a window and set fire to curtains and furnishings. According to plan, someone ruptured the building's gas line, and the leak ignited just as the intruders escaped. Again, the crowd blocked firefighters' access to the blaze.

Similar assaults that afternoon destroyed St. Michael's Roman Catholic Church, from which the priest barely escaped, and the Female Seminary that had been spared two days earlier. The mob

roared as the burning steeples toppled. The fires produced columns of smoke that were visible for miles. As the flames diminished, the fury of the nativists also seemed to subside. In a final flare-up, a remnant of the mob ransacked the home of Alderman Hugh Clark. The streets were empty before sundown.

In crowded and barricaded rooms in Kensington, many Irish Catholic families made plans to leave Philadelphia. Others argued that only by standing their ground could they ever make a home in America.

On Thursday morning, May 9, Mayor Scott convened a meeting in Independence Square to begin the process of restoring the public peace. In the three days of upheaval, 20 people had been killed, scores more injured and two Catholic churches and more than 50 Irish homes destroyed.

By acclamation, those present — many of whom had participated in the rioting — agreed to the appointment of special police units to patrol each neighborhood. Even the editors of the *Native American* voiced shock and regret: "No terms that we can use are able to express the deep reprobation that we feel for this iniquitous proceeding;

this wanton and uncalled-for desecration of the Christian altar."

Despite the general contrition and heightened security, isolated groups and individuals continued the campaign of anti-Catholic vandalism. Bishop Kenrick cancelled Sunday Mass throughout Philadelphia to avoid further confrontation. When posters boldly printed with the words "Fortunio and his Seven Gifted Servants" began appearing around the city, a rumor circulated that the strange slogan was a secret message from the Pope ordering Catholics to take up arms. The rumor died when a businessman revealed that the signs advertised a play coming soon to a local theatre.

The nativist/Irish conflict erupted again in Philadelphia later that summer. Organizers of the city's annual Independence Day celebration staged a procession honoring the widows and orphans of nativists who had died in the riots. The display rekindled bitter memories, and soon new suspicions arose that the Catholics were planning an uprising in the suburb of Southwark. Again the militia was called in, and the fighting that broke out was as fierce as that in Kensington. This time, the death toll reached 13.

Several months after these episodes, Philadelphia County complied with state law by repaying Catholics for damages incurred to their property in the mob violence. The riots of 1844 damaged the public image of the nativist movement, which would later seek new legitimacy in the political system. The establishment of a separate Catholic school system in Philadelphia solved the Bible problem but did little to heal the rift between the two communities. That process would take place some years later as nativists and Irish immigrants and soldiers of all stripes joined forces to preserve the federal union. ◆

Opposite page.
St. Michael's Church went up in flames, and the books from the St. Augustine's Church library fueled a bonfire in the street.

AT ISSUE

Majority Rule

We often describe our democracy as a system of "majority rule." When we hold elections to decide who will represent us in government, the choice of the largest number of voters is the winner. When those representatives debate issues in the student council or the state legislature or the national Congress, a similar vote determines the will of the majority.

Deciding by numbers is a practical way of handling differences. In a dictatorship, differences don't matter — only one person's opinion counts. At the other end of the spectrum, consensus means that every decision requires the agreement of everyone. This process works well in small groups, but on the state and federal level, it would make government move even more slowly than it does now. Majority rule lets a body get on with its business as soon as more than half of the participants are satisfied.

Our Constitution has established safeguards to ensure that majority rule doesn't take away the rights of minorities. The 14th Amendment (1868) guarantees to all Americans "the equal protection of the laws." This means that even though the majority shapes our laws by electing the lawmakers, the government must apply those laws to all people equally.

In theory, every citizen has a voice at the ballot box. But the principle of majority rule means that some voices don't get heard. At various times in our history, lack of minority representation in government has allowed the majority to abuse minority rights:

• In Charlestown, Mass., for example, in 1834, the town council included no Catholics. When the local Catholic Church applied for burial privileges — the same right that everyone else in town had — the elected council was able simply to refuse.

• Following the emancipation of the slaves — and passage of the 14th amendment — many all-white local and state governments enacted laws that restricted the rights of the black minority.

• During World War II, Japanese American citizens found their rights ignored because of the fears of the majority.

• In the 1990s, some towns and states passed measures legalizing discrimination against homosexuals.

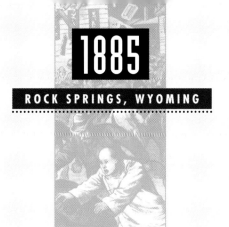

T O THOUSANDS OF CHINESE MEN in the 1850s, the prospect of striking it rich on "Gold Mountain" was worth the considerable risks of getting there. Many who journeyed to California during the Gold Rush left wives and children behind at a time of great uncertainty: A rebellion and a massive flood in Canton Province had recently killed thousands and devastated the economy.

Another hardship of emigrating was for-saking the graves of the ancestors. Other fami-ly members could continue to visit the

A Rumbling in the Mines

Language, culture and appearance all separated Chinese immigrants from their neighbors in 19th-century America. For many whites, these differences were cause enough for suspicion. But when the Chinese demonstrated their willingness to work for lower wages than their white counterparts, fear and distrust erupted into violence. The Chinese became victims not only of armed attacks but also of some of the most severe anti-immigration laws ever passed in this country.

cemeteries, but the spirits might still get angry at one who crossed the sea. And then there was the law to worry about: The penalty for leaving China was decapitation.

For a few Chinese prospectors, the California gold fields were a dream come true. Most, however, became laborers for large min-ing companies. Many remained after the boom to seek their fortunes in the towns and cities, where cooking, laundering and other service jobs paid 10 times the typical wage in China.

In 1862, a call went out for workers to build the western portion of a transcontinental railroad. Suppression of the Shoshoni tribe in Wyoming Territory had removed the last seri-ous obstacle to the government's right of way. As it turned out, not enough whites and free blacks applied to get the job done. Few Native Americans were interested, and a plan to use Confederate prisoners

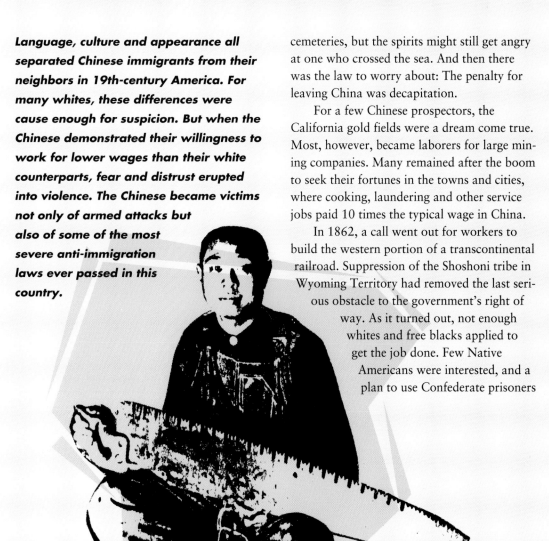

fell through when the Civil War ended.

Charles Crocker, chief contractor for the Central Pacific Railroad, had a Chinese manservant whose loyalty and capability he greatly admired. At Crocker's suggestion, the company hired 50 Chinese workers in California in 1865. The result was so favorable that Central Pacific began recruiting not only in the Western states but also in China.

By the peak period of construction three years later, the Chinese work force on the railroad numbered 12,000. The task of laying track across the rugged Sierra Nevada mountains was achieved by Chinese labor. Their jobs were difficult and dangerous. Winter storms, rock slides and accidents involving explosives cost 1,200 Chinese lives.

Completion of the project in 1869 sent the Chinese back into the cities. At a time of high unemployment, white workers resented foreign competition for scarce jobs. An anti-Chinese campaign, fueled by the newly emerging labor movement, spread rapidly through the West.

State and local governments introduced special taxes and regulations designed to harass the Chinese community. A California law prohibited Chinese from testifying against whites in court. Citizens of San Francisco held a rally in 1870 to protest Chinese immigration, and a mob in Los Angeles the following year murdered 23 Chinese. The Panic of 1873, which closed many businesses and factories nationwide, heightened racial tensions even further. Nevertheless, visions of wealth lured record numbers of Chinese to America during this period.

It was this teeming labor market that Union Pacific Railroad tapped when some of its white workers threatened to close the company's coal mines. Union Pacific had built the

> *Union Pacific openly favored Chinese workers over whites because the Chinese refused to join unions.*

Right. For the mostly Chinese work crews, the task of building the railroad continued through treacherous winters in the High Sierra.

Far right. Increasing employment of Chinese miners throughout the Western U.S. created resentment among whites.

eastern portion of the new railroad — from Omaha, Neb., to Promontory, Utah — and in the process had acquired extensive government land grants in mineral-rich Wyoming. By mining the coal deposits on its property, the railroad could meet its own fuel requirements and turn a handsome profit on the surplus coal.

In the snowy autumn of 1875, coal miners for the company at Rock Springs, Wyoming Territory, began planning a strike to protest a 20 percent pay cut. Railroad officials knew that one timely strike could stop a hundred locomotives on their tracks, so they contrived a threat of their own: If the plan went ahead, the most-

ly English and Irish strikers would be fired and replaced with Chinese laborers. When the strike occurred as scheduled, a train brought in 150 fresh recruits from Sacramento's Chinatown.

The arrival of the strikebreakers went peacefully, perhaps because two companies of U.S. Army troops had been assigned to Rock Springs a few days earlier after somebody shot at a mine boss. In a single day, railroad carpenters threw together a cluster of cabins that quickly became known as "Hong Kong." The new residents later used scrap lumber, packing crates and smashed tin cans to expand their company quarters.

Under federal guard, the Chinese laborers descended into the mines. Union Pacific dismissed 99 white miners who took part in the strike. Fifty whites remained on the payroll, outnumbered 3 to 1 by the Chinese. By mid-winter, the Rock Springs mines were operating again at their former capacity. Strikers who offered to resume work at the lower wage were handed one-way rail passes east to Omaha. The company's intentions were clear: It would tolerate no risk of future work stoppages.

Union Pacific, like many employers across the West, openly favored Chinese workers over whites because the Chinese refused to join unions. By the standards of their home country, the Chinese found American wages more than generous. In fact, most of the Chinese who came to America in the mid-19th century never intended to stay: After working and saving for a few years, they would return home wealthy by the standards of their countrymen. Because of these intentions, they were considered "sojourners" rather than immigrants.

While the anti-Chinese movement gained momentum in the cities, white workers in remote Rock Springs kept their hostility to themselves. The two racial segments of the community, in fact, kept almost everything to themselves. To the whites, the Chinese were merely alien pawns in the company's game. The sojourners, on the other hand, had little interest in the permanent residents of their "temporary" home.

Like its urban counterparts, the

DOCUMENT ▸

Out by Law

In 1879, the State of California adopted the following provisions in its constitution to exclude the Chinese. These sections were not repealed until 1952.

SECTION 2. No corporation now existing or hereafter formed under the laws of this State, shall, after the adoption of this Constitution, employ, directly or indirectly, in any capacity, any Chinese or Mongolian. The Legislature shall pass such laws as may be necessary to enforce this provision.

SECTION 3. No Chinese shall be employed on any State, county, municipal, or other public work, except in punishment for crime.

SECTION 4 *(in part).* The Legislature shall delegate all necessary power to the incorporated cities and towns of this State for the removal of Chinese without the limits of such cities and towns, or for their location within prescribed portions of those limits, and it shall also provide the necessary legislation to prohibit the introduction into this State of Chinese after the adoption of this Constitution.

makeshift Chinatown, or "Hong Kong," of Rock Springs was an island of Chinese culture where residents could trade and worship and practice medicine in their native style. Most of the food they ate came from Asia by way of San Francisco. For some members of the community, the imported culture even included opium-smoking. Membership in social groups called clans actively linked individuals with family and friends in other American cities and back home in China.

Whites both encouraged Chinese separatism and resented it. On the one hand, the Chinese were visibly and culturally more "different" from the European majority than the Scots and the Germans and the Italians were from each other. On the other hand, the bustling prosperity of the typical Chinatown struck onlookers as unfair and even dangerous. By 1882, national sentiment against the Chinese ran so high that Congress passed the Chinese Exclusion Act prohibiting further immigration.

Strict, voluntary segregation of the races at Rock Springs served Union Pacific's goal of keeping out organized labor. The company, by law, couldn't exclude white workers altogether, but it could give preferential treatment to the Chinese. All workers received the same pay for every bushel of coal they dug, but whites were typically assigned to the spots that were most difficult to dig.

In the summer of 1884, a new union from the East called the Knights of Labor began organizing railroad workers in the Rockies. Union fever soon spread to the mines — except for those at Rock Springs. Union Pacific miners elsewhere staged a strike in October 1884, their first in nine years. Among their demands was the dismissal of the Rock Springs Chinese. White miners at Rock Springs showed support for the union by setting fire to a machine shop and demolishing a ventilation fan. It was rumored that some of them had secretly joined the railroad workers' union.

The vandalism marked the first time violence had erupted in Rock Springs over the

Above. Railroad company carpenters built the wooden cabins of "Hong Kong" in a single day.

Opposite page. Anti-Chinese demonstrations like this one in San Francisco rocked many cities of the West in the 1870s and '80s.

"The Chinese Must Go!"

The Rock Springs Massacre was one of many outbreaks of anti-Chinese violence in the late 19th century. Even many newly arrived European immigrants joined in the cry, "The Chinese must go!" On October 24, 1871, a white mob stormed through the Chinese section of Los Angeles, shooting, hanging or stabbing to death 23 Chinese men. One prominent doctor in the community pled for his life in English and Spanish while rioters stripped him and chopped off his fingers to steal his rings.

When the Exclusion Act of 1882 failed to solve the "Chinese problem," anti-Chinese sentiment grew. The violence at Rock Springs in 1885 sparked eruptions of hate across the West:

• Angry whites drove Chinese residents out of nearly 30 California towns, and expulsions occured on a lesser scale in New Mexico, Utah and Montana.

• At Orofino, Idaho, white townsmen jailed five Chinese men on charges of murder and hanged them without trial.

• One hundred Chinese in an Alaskan outpost were jammed onto a fishing boat and forced out to sea.

• Washington Territory (now Washington state) was the scene of widespread racial violence. In the Squak Valley, a mob that included two Native Americans attacked a group

Chinese issue. In three months, the strike ended with the company refusing to meet any of the white workers' demands. Although it allowed the strikers to return to work, Union Pacific prohibited any further hiring of whites. Attacks on Chinese flared around the region during that summer, and the company decided to eliminate all its white railroad crews. The stage was set for confrontation.

It started underground, in Rock Springs Mine Number Six. On September 1, 1885, two white miners and four Chinese quarreled over their assigned locations for

digging. The next morning, two of the sojourners reported to work early, although it was a Chinese holiday. As they had been instructed to do, they set explosives to loosen the coal. Shortly after the blast, the two whites appeared on the scene and complained that the Chinese had stolen their spot.

One of the Chinese began insulting one of the whites and struck at him with a coal pick. A fight broke out, quickly attracting miners of both races. When a sojourner swung his pick into a white man's stomach, other whites tackled the assailant and used

of Chinese farm workers who had just retired to their tents for the night. Three Chinese men died. The rest were chased away and their camp destroyed.

• Through the fall and winter of 1885, white citizens of Tacoma, Seattle and other Washington cities organized massive anti-Chinese campaigns. All the residents of Tacoma's Chinatown were sent away by train. In February 1886, the forced evacuation

of Chinese from Seattle by steamship created such pandemonium that the governor called in federal troops.

Anti-Chinese violence subsided after a second, more restrictive Exclusion Act was signed into law by Pres. Grover Cleveland on Sept. 21, 1888. While the original act excluded only "Chinese laborers," the new one targeted (with a few exemptions) "all persons of the Chinese race."

DOCUMENT

Chinese Exclusion Act

The following law was enacted by the U.S. Congress on May 6, 1882. It was revised in 1888 and remained in effect until 1943, when Congress repealed it as a gesture of friendship to China during World War II.

Whereas, in the opinion of the Government of the United States the coming of Chinese laborers to this country endangers the good order of certain localities within the territory thereof: Therefore,

Be it enacted by the Senate and House of Representatives of the United States of America in Congress assembled, That from and after the expiration of ninety days next after the passage of this act, the coming of Chinese laborers to the United States be, and the same is hereby, suspended; and during such suspension it shall not be lawful for any Chinese laborer to come, or having so come after the expiration of said ninety days, to remain within the United States. ...

SECTION 14. That hereafter no State court or court of the United States shall admit Chinese to citizenship.

SEATTLE RESTAURANT
Under New Management.

The Traveling Public will find this the Cheapest and Best House in Town.

No Chinese Employed
About the House.

Meals, 25c.
Single Rooms, 25c.

A. J. TICE, Proprietor,

No. 8 Mill Street,   SEATTLE, W. T.

OAK RESTAURANT,
SHORT & STEVENS, PROPRIETORS,

Washington Street,   Near Commercial,
(Opp. Judge Lyon's Court.)

EMPLOYS WHITE HELP ONLY.

Table Always Supplied with the Best that the Market can Afford.

Twenty-one Meal Tickets for $4.50.

Above. Businesses during this period often complied with the racial prejudices of their customers.

the pick to open his skull. The mayhem continued for a half-hour before the foremen arrived.

News of the fight scuttled through the coal camp. Many whites exited the shafts and refused to go back in. A large group collected guns, knives, axes and bats from their cabins and gathered on the train tracks near Mine Number Six. A committee of concerned citizens persuaded them to put down their weapons, but the mob moved through town shouting, "White men, fall in!"

The bell clamored atop the Knights of Labor hall. At a special meeting, men from Number Six and other mines discussed the morning's incident and voted to convene again at 6 p.m. The crowd adjourning to the saloons of Front Street quickly became so unruly that the proprietors cleared them out at noon. A few Chinese on their way home for lunch were

surprised by angry whites who shouted racist slogans and pelted the sojourners with coal and bricks. Further on, warning shots whistled past a few Chinese heads.

Because of the holiday, many Chinese had stayed at home. They heard reports of the trouble, but most fully expected the company to step in and protect them as it always had. Now each passing hour raised more doubts. Early in the afternoon, Chinatown leaders hoisted an emergency flag, warning everyone to remain inside.

A rumor that federal troops had been summoned agitated the white mob. More than 100 men — trainmen and assorted drifters as well as coal miners — headed toward Hong Kong. Along the way, they paused at a gun shop long enough to purchase the entire inventory of bullets and shotgun shells. The army of spectators that followed close behind included women and children.

Two bridges over Bitter Creek connected Hong Kong with Rock Springs. Three men crossed the first bridge to give the Chinese a warning: Be out of town in an hour. The sojourners could see the mob now in the distance, but they still expected the company to intercede. Among the whites, the empty streets provoked a new rumor: that the Chinese were armed and prepared to defend their houses.

The crowd lost patience before the hour was up. In two groups they crossed the creek and sealed off the bridges. One group marched up the hill and opened fire on a pumphouse and coal shed where some sojourners were hiding. Lo Sun Chi ran out of the pumphouse and took a bullet in his back. Liu Tieh Pa made a fatal dash toward the railroad bridge. A third man, Liu Chiu Pu, fell dead from a shot through the neck. On the opposite creek bank, the onlookers were cheering.

The mob reassembled at the edge of Chinatown proper and hastily mapped out its attack. Squads of 8 or 10 dispersed into the maze-like streets and passageways. The rioters smashed windows, rammed doors and herded the frightened residents into the streets, showing little mercy for women or children. The safest route of escape was southeast across the creek toward Burning Mountain. Many of the

Chinese were barefoot. Most fled with no more possessions than the thin cotton work suits on their backs. The rioters stole any visible jewelry or other valuables and beat or shot or released the owners as they saw fit.

Several women participated in the violence. A Mrs. Osborn, who ran a laundry, shot two sojourners and later picked through stacks of shirts and pants in the shop of a dead Chinese laundryman. On the street, another woman carrying a baby punched a Chinese man in the face.

Dr. Edward Murray, a local physician, charged to and fro on horseback, shouting "Shoot them down!" After the first wave of the assault concluded, it was Murray's idea to go back and set fire to what was left. This included the bodies of the dead and

Left. Denver was the scene of another violent attack on Chinese workers.

Below. The massacre at Rock Springs left 25 Chinese miners dead and hundreds homeless.

wounded. As Hong Kong went up in flames, a few more Chinese scrambled out of hiding, their heads wrapped in blankets to protect them from the smoke. Here and there, kegs of gunpowder used for blasting coal exploded inside the cabins. Each time this happened, the white spectators let loose a roar.

Around a bend in the creek, 600 sojourners huddled on a hillside in the cold and watched their homes burn. The foul black cloud that settled over the valley brought an early dusk. As the first fires died, rioters stirred the rubble, looking for stashes of gold. One group returned to Rock Springs and went to the houses of the three officials responsible for hiring the Chinese. One was out of town already, and the other two left on the next train. By now, the county sheriff had made it in from Green River, but his efforts to gather a posse failed.

In the days that followed, trains thundered through Rock Springs without stopping. Newspapers around the country carried accounts of the massacre that killed 25 Chinese miners. Reports estimated that more than that number perished afterward from the cold. One family driven into the surrounding scrubland that night got lost. The baby died of exposure in just a few hours. The mother fell ill and died the next day. The father watched the wolves circling as long as he could stand it and then took his own life with his pistol.

Of the more than 100 people who openly participated in the violence at Rock Springs, 16 were arrested. A grand jury called to investigate the massacre returned no indictments. Some Chinese returned to the mines, but Union Pacific reversed its hiring practices and gradually replaced the Chinese with whites. ◆

Dr. Edward Murray, a local physician, charged to and fro on horseback, shouting "Shoot them down!"

Right. At the suggestion of Dr. Murray, rioters burned the abandoned "Hong Kong" district to the ground.

Opposite page.
The Chinese miners who returned to Rock Springs lived in boxcars until new quarters could be provided.

The Bottom Line?

In times of economic hardship and high unemployment, people in communities often come together to help each other. During the Great Depression of the 1930s, many farm families took in the homeless or let hoboes stay in their barns. Churches and civic groups operated soup kitchens. City neighborhoods held dances and other free social events. People tightened their belts and endured the hard times together.

But a troubled economy can also tear people apart. Competition for scarce jobs and housing can narrow our perspective: The world and our feelings about it can shrink to the scale of our next meal or our child's worn-out shoes.

As a result, our sense of community and loyalty also narrows. This is especially true where differences like race and language and religion have never really been bridged. Under the pressure of economic uncertainty, these differences become more threatening. The difference between "us" and "them" can seem like a matter of survival. It can stir us to hate.

White company owners brought Chinese workers to Rock Springs to break a strike by whites. These officials knew full well that they were setting up a racial conflict. The self-sufficiency of the Chinese community only angered white miners more. But who could have bridged such a gap under these circumstances? From the outset, the situation was marked for disaster.

Our laws today make it more difficult for anyone to exploit racial divisions for economic gain. But the fault-lines in our society can still rupture under economic stress, as victims of hardship search for someone to blame. This happened in the Midwest in the 1980s, when low crop prices and high production costs forced many farmers out of business. At farm auctions around the region, posters and fliers and public speakers blamed the crisis on Jews in the financial industry.

Also during the 1980s, sales of Japanese automobiles in the United States skyrocketed while the U.S. auto industry suffered a decline. High unemployment in Detroit and other automotive centers set off a wave of "Japan-bashing." Some angry workers and consumers expressed their frustration by vandalizing Japanese-made cars.

One June night in 1982, two unemployed white auto workers got into an argument with a man named Vincent Chin in a Detroit bar. Chin was a Detroit native, and Chinese-American, but the angry strangers mistook him for Japanese. When he left, they followed him to a nearby McDonald's and beat him with a baseball bat. Four days later, Vincent Chin died.

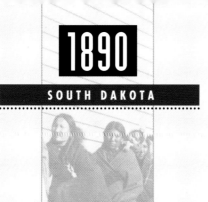

ONE DAY WHEN HE WAS 14, a boy named Slow followed his father and some other Hunkpapa Sioux warriors on a raid against the neighboring Crow people. This was around 1845, in what is now South Dakota. The boy carried only a stick in his hand, but he rode straight toward a Crow warrior who was aiming an arrow at him and knocked the warrior to the ground.

For Slow's bravery, his father gave him a new name: Tatanka Yotanka, or Sitting Bull,

Ghost Dance at Wounded Knee

The massive Indian removals of the 1830s marked the end of the first phase of Indian conquest. Later, as the United States set its sights across the entire continent, there was no "outside" land to which Indians could be banished. Instead, the tribes were corraled inside the fixed borders of reservations — mostly barren patches of land that the whites hadn't yet found a use for. While the Civil War was raging over the destiny of the slaves, the Indian Wars signaled the fate of another people. The contest reached its costly climax in 1890, on a South Dakota Sioux reservation called Pine Ridge.

after the solitary buffalo that came to the father one night as a sign. Sitting Bull earned membership in the elite Strong Heart Society of warriors before he turned 17. He later became the society's leader.

Sitting Bull came of age during a time of sweeping change for his people. Gathering on the horizon was an enemy much more powerful than the Crows. The U.S. government was starting to view the Great Plains as more than just a dumping ground for the eastern Indians. California gold fever brought herds of fortune-seekers over the grasslands. Railroads followed, sprouting supply depots and settlements along the way. Now the Plains tribes saw their worlds shifting and shrinking as the worlds of the Choctaws and the Cherokees and others had two decades before. The government's policy toward the Indians amounted to a war strategy: Divide and conquer.

Sitting Bull was determined to

resist. In 1868, he led a group of Sioux who refused to sign a treaty confining the tribe to a reservation. He knew that such treaties had often been broken, and he also knew that, within such narrow boundaries, his people's way of life would end. Sitting Bull's defiance inspired thousands of Indians from many Plains tribes to join the cause.

It wasn't long before the Army, fulfilling the Indians' worst fears, violated the Sioux treaty to prospect for gold in the Black Hills. Lt. Col. George Armstrong Custer was the leader of this expedition. In 1876, after the Sioux refused to sell the Black Hills, the government launched attacks against Sitting Bull's branch and declared all of the reservation-dwellers prisoners of war.

On June 17 of that year, Sitting Bull, Crazy Horse and other fugitive Sioux surprised an Army unit at Rosebud Creek in southeastern Montana and forced it to retreat. Not far to the west, along the Little Bighorn River, the victorious Indians stopped to hunt awhile and rest their horses. Here Sitting Bull performed the Sun Dance, a special ritual for bringing on visions. Afterwards he described what he had seen: government soldiers dropping out of the sky like grasshoppers.

The following week, Custer's 7th Cavalry approached the sprawling riverside camp. No one knows why the commander ordered his men to charge the Indians before the expected reinforcements arrived. Of more than 200 U.S. troops and their mounts, only one horse, named Comanche, survived the resulting slaughter. The incident lent a bitter flavor to the nation's centennial celebrations on July 4.

Sitting Bull's legions knew that they would pay for the blow they had dealt the Army. The gathered tribes went their separate ways, some onto the open plains, others onto reservations. Sitting Bull kept his faith that the Indians could hold out against the white man's greed. Meanwhile, the government forcibly

> *The government forcibly "purchased" nine million acres from the reservation Sioux.*

Opposite page. Sitting Bull toured the U.S. and Canada with William F. Cody's Wild West Show from 1885 to 1887.

"purchased" nine million acres from the reservation Sioux.

For five more years, Sitting Bull and his people wandered in the wilderness, resisting U.S. demands for their surrender. They sought refuge in Canada but finally, on the promise of a pardon for their leader, turned themselves in at Fort Buford, Dakota Territory, on July 19, 1881. The government agents broke their word and arrested Sitting Bull. He was held in military prison for two years before being released into the custody of Interior

IN CONTEXT

Buffalo Bill and Sitting Bull

Like Sitting Bull, William F. Cody demonstrated his bravery and skill as a warrior early in life. He learned to wrangle horses and fight Indians as a boy in Kansas. During the Civil War, he served as a teenage scout for the 9th Kansas Cavalry in its campaigns against the Comanches and Kiowas.

When the Union Pacific Railway began laying its tracks across the continent, Cody found work as a buffalo hunter supplying the huge construction crews with meat. He earned his nickname by reportedly killing 4,280 of the animals in an eight-month stretch.

At the time the Civil War ended, the buffalo on the Plains numbered around 12 million. To the 31 Indian tribes of the region, these animals were a sacred gift of food, clothing and shelter. The white man saw them differently.

Professional marksmen like Buffalo Bill were followed by tourists who fired on grazing herds for sport. The discovery of a commercial process for making buffalo leather spurred the slaughter of more than 9 million head in the early 1870s. By the turn of the century, the entire buffalo population of the U.S. would be slashed to fewer than 50.

While Sitting Bull (named for a buffalo) was fighting for the rights of his people to live as they always had, Buffalo Bill Cody

Department agents at Standing Rock Reservation.

Through vivid, often exaggerated newspaper accounts, Sitting Bull's exploits had brought him international fame. The government arranged public appearances for the captive chief in 15 U.S. cities during 1884. The following year, he joined Buffalo Bill Cody's traveling Wild West Show *(see sidebar)*.

Sitting Bull returned to the reservation in 1887. The government was trying to force the Sioux to sell more land, so the chief took up his old cause of resistance.

Within a couple of years, the government had won again and divided the reduced reservation into six parts. Life for the Sioux grew more and more miserable. Diseases swept through the reservations like winds of death. Carrots and potatoes withered in the hard ground.

Around this same time, a new religious movement was spreading among Indian tribes all across the west. Far away in

and others were helping to make that impossible. With the herds depleted, life as the Sioux and the Cheyenne and the Arapaho and the Pawnee and their neighbors knew it came to an end.

On July 17, 1876, just a few weeks after Custer's Last Stand at Little Bighorn, Buffalo Bill gave white Americans a taste of revenge against the Indians by taking the scalp of Yellow Hair, the son of a Cheyenne chief. This deed was not only a brazen act of warfare but also a canny business maneuver.

Between Indian fights, Cody had often performed in stage plays about the West. After his decisive triumph over Yellow Hair, re-enactments of the encounter became the centerpiece of a nationwide theatrical tour. The buffalo hunter and Indian fighter had become America's most popular showman.

In 1883, Cody organized a combination circus, rodeo and traveling museum called the Wild West Show, which became an overnight sensation. In 1885, he had little trouble persuading the reservation agents to let him take Sitting Bull off their hands.

This arrangement was conducted at least partially on Sitting Bull's terms. He asked for and received $50 a month payment and the full proceeds from posing for photographs. Other theatrical agents had used captured Indians as objects of mockery, but Cody treated Sitting Bull with dignity. Instead of leading other Indians into staged defeats, the Sioux chief rode his horse silently and alone into the arena. Although audiences hissed and booed, newspapers around the country and in Canada reported that the image of the solitary leader inspired a general sense of awe. Behind the scenes, Sitting Bull enjoyed the company of the other performers, especially the sure-shot Annie Oakley, whom he offered to adopt.

The respect that Cody showed Sitting Bull during his two years in the Wild West Show helped to forge a surprising friendship between the two former enemies. After Sitting Bull's death, many chiefs followed his lead and took advantage of the relative freedom the Wild West Show offered.

How the West Was Lost

A writer named John L. O'Sullivan predicted in 1845 "the fulfillment of our manifest destiny to overspread the continent allotted by Providence." He sensed, as many other Americans did, the unfolding of a divine plan for the country's expansion. Just four years later, the discovery of gold in California turned "manifest destiny" into a stampede. Forty-niners (men seeking their fortunes in the gold fields in 1849) flocked west by the thousands. San Francisco was their boomtown. Calls for statehood came swift and loud.

With the admission of California to the Union in 1850, the western border of the U.S. leaped from Iowa and Missouri and Texas to the Pacific in a single bound. In more than just a political sense, the Indians in between were surrounded. The U.S. Senate imposed the following conditions in its treaty with the Western Shoshoni in 1863.

The telegraph and overland stage lines having been established and operated by companies under the authority of the United States through a part of the Shoshonee country, it is expressly agreed that the same may be continued without hindrance, molestation, or injury from the people

(Continued on page 62)

(Continued from page 61)

How the west was lost

of said bands. .... And further, it being understood that provision had been made by the government of the United States for the construction of a railway from the plains west to the Pacific ocean, it is stipulated by the said bands that the said railway or its branches may be located, constructed, and operated, and without molestation from them, through any portion of country claimed or occupied by them.

It is further agreed by the parties hereto, that the Shoshonee country may be explored and prospected for gold and silver, or other minerals; and when mines are discovered, they may be worked, and mining and agricultural settlements formed, and ranches established whenever they may be required.

...

The said bands agree that whenever the President of the United States shall deem it expedient for them to abandon the roaming life, which they now lead, and become herdsmen or agriculturalists, he is hereby authorized to make such reservations for their use as he may deem necessary within the country above described; and they do also hereby agree to remove their camps to such reservations as he may indicate, and to reside and remain therein.

Nevada, a Paiute Indian farmer named Wovoka was telling his people about a vision he'd had in which all the ancestors and buffalo rose from the dead, restoring the old Indian way of life forever. In a time of increasing pressure from whites, Indians listened eagerly to this message of deliverance. They began performing a dance that Wovoka said would make the vision come true.

Wovoka's movement, which whites called the Ghost Dance, combined earlier Indian prophecies with elements of Christianity that Wovoka had picked up from missionaries and white neighbors. From the Mormons, for example, he may have borrowed the idea of sacred garments that protect the wearer from harm. Stories circulated that Wovoka himself was the new Messiah, Jesus Christ returned to save the Indian people.

When Sitting Bull heard about the energy and excitement that the Ghost Dance was stirring among other tribes, he thought about his own desperate people. They were practically starving on government rations, and the government had told them that they could no longer supplement their diets by hunting game. The winter ahead promised to be a grim one on the carved-up Sioux reservations.

Sitting Bull felt the new religion might at least give his people something to hope for. In October 1890, he invited some Sioux from another area to come teach the Ghost Dance. The religion quickly attracted many followers with its promise of Indian victory and glory. Sioux men, women and children were soon so busy dancing in the snow that no work was getting done. Houses, schools and stores stood empty. The dancers claimed that the special shirts they wore would repel the white man's bullets.

The whites had laws to protect their own freedom of religion, but the Ghost Dance frightened them. The religious frenzy seemed more a portent of rebellion than a broken culture's desperate attempt to make sense of its collapsing world. Newspapers across the country fanned the flames of suspicion. In mid-November, Pres. Benjamin

Harrison directed the Secretary of War to suppress "any threatened out break among the Indians." The Indian Bureau in Washington ordered its reservation agents to telegraph the names of suspected troublemakers. One of the names on this list was Sitting Bull's.

Because of his celebrated history, the government knew it had to carry out Sitting Bull's arrest with extreme caution. The general in charge enlisted the aid of Buffalo Bill Cody, who agreed to use his friendship, along with a few gifts, to coax Sitting Bull's surrender. Cody travelled to the reservation, but at the last minute a nervous agent telegraphed the President and convinced him to cancel the plan.

The Ghost Dancers had been assembling in the Badlands on Pine Ridge Reservation. On December 11, Sitting Bull asked for permission to go there. Now the government believed it could justify having him arrested.

Forty-three armed reservation police surrounded his cabin before dawn on December 15. A crowd of Ghost Dancers gathered in the cold. When Sitting Bull came out, they tried to prevent his capture, but in the scuffle a policeman shot Sitting Bull through the brain.

News of Sitting Bull's death shook the Sioux like a lightning bolt. Part of his band turned to Chief Big Foot for guidance. Big Foot was another Sioux resistance leader who had been hiding out with some supporters in the Badlands. He believed that Chief Red Cloud at Pine Ridge, who was

Above left. Sitting Bull hoped his own fame would call attention to the plight of his people.

Above right and below. Ration day at Pine Ridge brought hundreds of Sioux women to stand in line for bacon, cornmeal, flour, coffee and sugar. In 1890, the government cut rations by 20 percent.

"A Superior and Civilized Nation"

In 1913, members of the Pueblo tribe challenged the degree of control that Congress exercised over tribal affairs. The U.S. Supreme Court issued the following statements in its decision (United States v. Sandoval).

Always living in separate and isolated communities, adhering to primitive modes of life, largely influenced by superstition and fetishism, and chiefly governed according to crude customs inherited from their ancestors, [the Pueblos] are essentially a simple, uninformed and inferior people. ... As a superior and civilized nation, [the U.S. government has both] the power and the duty of exercising a fostering care and protection over all dependent Indian communities within its borders.

experienced in dealing with whites, offered the best chance for protection from the government. So he set out to take his followers there.

The refugees had little food. Many of them walked barefoot on the frozen ground, while others used torn strips of blanket to bind their feet. Sleet covered their clothes and gave them a glassy shine. Big Foot developed a deep rattling cough. His nose bled frequently, and he refused to eat. On December 25, he directed his men to kill the youngest horses and ration the meat.

When cavalry troops intercepted the party three days later, the exhausted Indians raised tattered flour sacks as truce flags. Big Foot formally surrendered and received an ambulance wagon to ride in. The troops then herded their captives — 120 men and 230 women and children — toward the Army camp at Wounded Knee Creek. The shoes on the soldiers' horses rang out against the earth, which was hard as iron.

Although the Indians had surrendered and were clearly in no position to put up a fight, the situation at the camp was tense.

Two cavalry units guarded the Sioux tepees, and Hotchkiss machine guns (with a range of two miles) sat atop a nearby rise. By morning, more guns had been added.

After a breakfast of Army rations, the Indians were ordered to give up all weapons they were hiding. A few rifles were handed over, but not enough to satisfy the officers. Soldiers herded the Sioux into a cluster and searched the tepees, collecting any knives, tools or guns they could find. They searched the women and made them unwrap their babies in the cold.

At the edge of the crowd, a medicine man named Yellow Bird lifted his arms and started a Ghost Dance. As he danced, he sang — about strong Sioux hearts and

about soldiers' bullets falling harmless on the prairie. The people listened. Yellow Bird's strange chant worried and angered the officers. A quick search of some Indians turned up two more rifles. An attempt to seize a third one caused it to fire.

The single gunshot set the soldiers in motion. They raised their rifles, took aim and began firing. Some of the Indians grabbed hatchets and knives from the surrendered pile. Many fell dead. Others, including Big Foot, died where they had been sitting under blankets to keep warm. A few stray Army bullets killed soldiers. Then the hell-bursts of the Hotchkiss guns tore holes in the tepees. Thunder echoed. The blood of women and children stained the ground.

Soldiers cried, "Remember Custer!" and kept firing. The Hotchkiss guns now fixed their aim on a ravine where some Indians hid. Most of those who fled were hunted down and shot.

When the guns went silent, the soldiers removed their own 25 dead. A blizzard that night laid a clean blanket over the corpses of 290 Sioux. ◆

IN CONTEXT

Wounded Knee Revisited

In 1973, Pine Ridge Reservation again became a site of confrontation between Native Americans and the U.S. government. On February 27, armed members of the American Indian Movement (AIM), numbering around 200, seized control of the town of Wounded Knee.

They proclaimed themselves the "Independent Oglala Sioux Nation" and demanded that the government implement changes in tribal leadership and review all Indian treaties as well as the treatment of native peoples in general.

Federal marshals immediately surrounded the hamlet. In the nine-day siege that followed, two Oglala Sioux were killed and a federal marshal was wounded. On May 8, the government promised to negotiate on the group's demands. AIM members surrendered their weapons and ended the standoff.

In response to this and other protests by Native Americans, Congress in 1975 passed the Indian Self-Determination and Education Assistance Act, which paid tribes to take over certain services from the federal government. Some groups, charging that the act had little substance, predicted a much longer struggle to overcome the government's former policy of Indian "termination."

Opposite page, above. Big Foot, wounded in the first round of gunfire on Dec. 29, 1890, was shot dead later in the morning.

Opposite page, below. On Jan. 1 and 2, 1891, the frozen corpses were buried in a mass grave.

Left. Sacred Heart Catholic Church was one of several buildings seized during the Oglala Sioux occupation of Wounded Knee in February 1973.

The Ballad of Leo Frank

The myth of a Jewish conspiracy is an old one that thrives on a mix of economic insecurities and cultural prejudice. During the recession of the 1980s, white supremacist groups recruited new members by arguing that Jews in business and government were responsible for the problems of working-class Protestant whites. In the 1990s, Nation of Islam leader Louis Farrakhan used similar reasoning to pronounce Jews the enemy of African Americans.

In Georgia in 1913, the Jewish conspiracy myth found its focus in the murder of Mary Phagan, a 13-year-old girl who worked for a Jewish factory superintendent named Leo Frank.

EARLY ONE SUNDAY MORNING while making his rounds, the night watchman at the National Pencil Company found the body of a teenage girl in the basement coal bin. Soot so thoroughly covered the corpse that the police, working by lantern-light, at first didn't realize the dead girl was white.

Before her death in Atlanta on April 26, 1913, Mary Phagan was one of the invisibles — that small army of children whose nimble hands and small needs made them excellent industrial workers. About to turn 14, she worked 10-hour days for 12 cents an hour in the pencil factory. It was Mary's job to attach the copper caps that held the erasers on the pencil shafts.

The police quickly arrested several suspects in the murder. One was Newt Lee, the night watchman, who was black. Another was a black man named Jim Conley, who worked at the pencil factory as a sweeper and was seen washing blood from a shirt shortly after the incident. A third was the white

factory superintendent, Leo Frank. According to police detectives, they had found bloodstains and hair of the victim near Frank's office.

Hugh M. Dorsey was Atlanta's prosecuting attorney at this time. Dorsey hoped to use his current position as a stepping-stone to a state or national political career. Two recent failures to convict accused murderers had damaged his reputation. He believed that nailing the killer of Mary Phagan would restore his popularity and help him realize his dream.

The police also needed a conviction, in order to preserve the public trust. These were uneasy times in Atlanta and cities like it around the South. Racial tensions were erupting into riots, such as the one that rocked Atlanta in 1906. Descriptions of ongoing police brutality and nightmarish prison conditions stirred both outrage and fear, even among law-abiding citizens.

There were serious economic problems as well. Recent droughts and the boll weevil had crippled Georgia's cotton agricul-

ture and forced farm families into the cities to find work. There, they lived in over-crowded and unsanitary slum apartments. Low wages and the high cost of urban living made it necessary for women and even children to labor from dawn to dusk in the mills.

These circumstances placed tremendous strain on the uprooted farming class. Working conditions in the huge factories and assembly shops were dreadful and dangerous. Drunks and prostitutes roamed the city streets. Young girls were often harassed or even raped at work.

What made these wretched conditions seem even worse to the rural immigrants was the fact that many factory owners and supervisers were outsiders, typically from the North. Leo Frank, Mary's boss at the National Pencil Company, was an outsider on two counts — he was a "Yankee" and he was a Jew.

The rural people who came to work in Frank's factory carried long-held prejudices

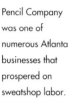

The National Pencil Company was one of numerous Atlanta businesses that prospered on sweatshop labor.

Mary Phagan

toward strangers of any kind. To these poverty-worn descendants of pioneers, the Jews were wealthy aliens who practiced mysterious rituals and rejected Jesus. Although he had married an Atlanta native, and his blood uncle had fought for the Confederacy, Leo Frank from Brooklyn would always be one of "them."

Atlanta had an old, established Jewish community, the largest in the South. Despite social barriers based on anti-Semitism, several Jews held public offices. But the new figure of the Jewish factory boss gave Protestant Christians new grounds for prejudice — economic exploitation.

As questioning of the three main suspects proceeded, the public raised an angry cry for justice — or, more accurately, for revenge. In this edgy atmosphere, the authorities became increasingly careless with their information. They released tantalizing half-truths to reporters, who filled in the gaps with hearsay. One policeman, for instance, claimed to have discovered Frank in the woods with a young girl a year earlier. By the time the officer admitted having confused Frank with someone else, the press had already moved on to the next "revelation."

The sensational murder story sent sales of all three Atlanta daily newspapers skyrocketing. Each attempted to outdo the other in dramatizing the case's details. In a bold publicity stunt, one paper raised money to bring in "the world's greatest detective" to compete with local police. Coverage of the murder, the investigation and the trial took Atlanta's press to new depths of yellow journalism.

Investigators soon lost interest in the night watchman. That left Conley and Frank. Given the social status of blacks in Atlanta in 1913 — not to mention the bloody shirt he was seen scrubbing — it might have appeared that Conley was a dead man. Far less provocation than the murder of a white girl had caused many black men to hang.

Almost from the outset, however, both the police and the press focused their attention on Frank. In fact, no one even sent Conley's shirt to a lab for testing. And an insurance agent who reported hearing a confession from Conley was told that no blacks were present at the factory on the day of the crime.

An explanation for the authorities' behavior can be found in a statement by the pastor of the Baptist church Mary attended: "This one old Negro would be poor atonement for the life of this innocent girl." In Leo Frank, a New York Jewish factory boss, white Protestant Atlantans found a demon "worthy to pay for the crime."

Little Mary Phagan was no longer invisible. She had become a symbol for everything

> *Leo Frank was an outsider on two counts — he was a "Yankee" and he was a Jew.*

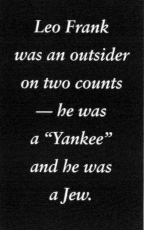

Leo Frank

that the Leo Franks of the world were coming to take away. One periodical later called her "a daughter of the people, ... of those who eat bread in the sweat of the face, and who, in so many instances are the chattel slaves of a sordid Commercialism that has no milk of human kindness in its heart of stone!"

At the pre-trial hearings, no one contradicted Frank's calm account of his own actions on April 26. But witness after witness came forth to cast doubt on his character. They described him as a flirt, a ladies' man, a pervert. In an appeal to a different prejudice, someone even suggested that he was a closet Catholic.

In late May, the prosecution released a series of four sworn statements from Conley. Each story was different. By the fourth statement, Conley was claiming that, on the afternoon of April 26, Frank asked him to attend to a girl that Frank had "let fall" against a machine in the work room. Conley said that he found the girl dead, and that Frank helped him carry her body to the basement by elevator.

Hugh Dorsey and the detectives took Conley to the factory and asked him to walk them through the events of the fateful day. Conley showed them where he first talked to Frank, where he found the girl and where they moved her.

As the elevator reached the bottom of the shaft, the investigators heard something being crushed underneath them. They discovered that it was a girl's umbrella. Dorsey must have hoped that no one would realize its significance: If the umbrella had been standing in the shaft undisturbed until now, then that proved that Conley was lying. He and Frank hadn't brought Mary Phagan down on the elevator.

Even without this evidence, the grand jury saw enough holes in Conley's statements to charge him with murder. But Dorsey persuaded them to indict Frank: The time was right for singling out a Jew.

The trial of Leo Frank opened on July 28, 1913, at the City Hall and dragged on for four scorching weeks. Each day, the crowd of spectators was so large and so agitated that 20 police officers were posted around the courtroom. Men standing in the

tall open windows shouted play-by-play commentary to the people outside. Street vendors sold refreshments, and on one occasion a bold youngster made good money indoors hawking sandwiches to those who didn't want to leave their seats during the lunch recess.

Dorsey built his case against Leo Frank on the testimony of Jim Conley. Outfitted in a new suit and fresh haircut, Conley reinforced his story with fresh allegations: that he frequently served as a "lookout" while Frank entertained female visitors in his office; that Frank wanted Mary Phagan to be one of those visitors; that when she rebuffed him, he killed her for it.

Conley's tale was so shocking that the judge dismissed all women and children from the courtroom. The omission of "unprintable" passages from the newspapers only heightened the public drama even more. Every chance he got, Dorsey raised questions about Frank's sex life, to underscore the defendant's image as a beast.

Dorsey knew that Frank's defense lawyers could be tough opponents if they wanted to. Amazingly, in this case they seemed distracted and careless. They permitted false evidence to go unchallenged. (Later analysis revealed that the "bloodstains" found near Frank's office, for example, were really spots of paint.) They hadn't even requested that the trial be moved out of Atlanta, although the local bias would have been obvious to anyone. At every turn, the courtroom thundered with cheers for Dorsey, boos for Frank. Each morning as the jury walked over from a nearby hotel, the crowd chanted, "Hang the Jew, or we'll hang you!"

The witnesses called to defend Frank were mostly Jews themselves, or Northern business associates of the accused. None of these was likely to sway a typical Atlanta jury. When Frank finally took the witness stand, his testimony was convincing, and many newspapers supported him. But, fortunately for Hugh Dorsey, the verdict wouldn't be decided by the press.

Frank's lawyers thought that the facts would speak for themselves, that Conley's

Each morning as the jury walked over from a nearby hotel, the crowd chanted, "Hang the Jew, or we'll hang you!"

Lucille Selig Frank, an Atlanta native, watched Hugh Dorsey rouse the city's hatred toward her husband.

deceit was obvious. They underestimated the power of the word 'Jew.'

In his closing argument, Dorsey praised well-known Jewish leaders and businessmen, in order to demonstrate his own lack of prejudice. Then he recited the names and deeds of notorious Jewish criminals. The Jews, he said, "rise to heights sublime, but they also sink to the lowest depths of degradation!"

Dorsey's sweeping indictment of the Jewish people held his audience spellbound. It was getting late, and Judge Leonard S. Roan knew what even ordinary Saturday nights were like in the rowdy streets of Atlanta. This was no ordinary Saturday. The judge decided that it was better to postpone the rest of Dorsey's closing argument until Monday than to let it end now and turn the crowd into a mob.

On Monday morning, August 25, Dorsey received a hero's welcome, and Judge Roan threatened to clear the courtroom. For three hours, the prosecutor hammered his point home: Leo Frank murdered Mary Phagan. "Guilty!" Dorsey shouted at precisely noon, and church bells chimed. Less than four hours later, the jury announced its agreement.

Outside the building, hats sailed into the air. Women wept in jubilation. Three strong men lifted Dorsey above the cheering multitude. At a local baseball field, officials posted the verdict on the scoreboard, and the fans went wild.

News of Frank's conviction swept the city, the state and the nation. The next day, Judge Roan sentenced Frank to hang. (Jim Conley's earlier conviction for accessory to murder brought him one year on a chain gang.) Frank's lawyers immediately began the process of appeals, none of which was to prove successful. Newspapers and magazines both locally and around the country issued calls for a re-trial.

Meanwhile, along Georgia's Main Streets, resentment of this national attention only fed a broader current of hate. An editor and veteran politician named Tom Watson was building a new reputation for himself as the white Southerners' champion. In his two journals, *Watson's Magazine* and *The Jeffersonian*, Watson turned the Frank case into a rallying cry against Northerners and against the factory system and particularly against Jews.

On October 2, 1914, more than a year after Frank's conviction, Jim Conley's lawyer

---

AT ISSUE

Scapegoats

In an old Jewish ritual, the high priest chose one goat each year — the scapegoat — to represent the sins of the whole nation. After a confession ceremony, the priest let the goat escape to carry the sins away.

Whenever something goes wrong around us, it's part of our human nature to look for someone to blame — to find a scapegoat. Sometimes we point at others to keep from being blamed ourselves. Usually, though, we just choose an easy target — someone we don't like much anyway, or someone it's easy to imagine doing wrong. If the wrong is big enough, we might look for a scapegoat "big enough" to properly pay for it.

For the white Christian majority of Atlanta

in 1913, the murder of Mary Phagan confirmed their worst fears about a rapidly changing world. In Leo Frank, a northern Jew, the community found a symbol for the factory system that was draining the life out of young girls. To many people, it didn't matter that Frank might be innocent. What mattered were his position and his background and what they stood for in the public mind.

Laying blame gives us the illusion of putting our world back in order. It can also relieve our own guilt, explain the unexplainable and provide an outlet for anger. But each time we lay blame mistakenly — each time we find a scapegoat — we only demean ourselves and put off addressing the real problem.

announced that his own client was Mary Phagan's murderer. Since he had already been tried and convicted of a lesser charge, the lawyer argued, Conley could not be tried again. But Frank could still be spared the noose.

Pressure mounted for Gov. John M. Slaton to commute Frank's death sentence. More than 100,000 letters poured in. Nine governors, including four Southern ones, urged executive clemency. Six state legislatures passed resolutions on Leo Frank's behalf. Across the nation, mass meetings, petitions and newspaper coupon drives voiced the support of a million people, 10,000 Georgians among them.

The clemency movement only fueled Tom Watson's fire. His editorials denouncing the "filthy, perverted Jew of New York" increased circulation of *The Jeffersonian* from 25,000 to 87,000. Jewish money, he said, was undermining the judicial system. At his suggestion, protesters held public rallies — one on the Georgia state capitol grounds. Watson even raised the possibility that a pardon for Frank might result in lynchings.

Gov. Slaton's term in office was almost over. He was one of the most popular governors in Georgia history. He could easily have left the Frank matter for his successor to deal with, but momentum for a decision was gathering. Judge Roan, a short time before his death, asked the governor to save Frank from an unjust execution. As more evidence of Frank's innocence surfaced, threats mounted against the governor's life.

Gov. Slaton later credited his wife with inspiring him to follow his conscience. As he spent a sleepless night on June 20, 1915, she told him, "I would rather be the widow of a brave and honorable man than the wife of a coward."

The governor secretly ordered the sheriff to transfer Leo Frank to the state prison farm at Milledgeville, 100 miles from Atlanta. Phone lines to the jail were disconnected. A decoy car idled in front of the building while authorities sneaked the prisoner out the back.

Slaton's announcement of his decision included a 10,000-word legal commentary, but one sentence summed up his feelings: "I would be a murderer if I allowed that man to hang."

The legions who had supported Frank cheered his victory. Others clamored that jus-tice had been undone. Across Georgia, people took to the streets, stringing up effigies of the governor and burning them. A Columbus man let his daughters shoot at a dummy hoisted in the air. "John M. Slaton, King of the Jews and Georgia's Traitor Forever" read a sign on an effigy in Marietta, Mary Phagan's hometown.

The "Marietta Vigilance Committee" distributed a flier to Jewish shopkeepers:

NOTICE
You are hereby notified to close up this business and quit Marietta by Saturday night … or else stand the consequences. We mean to rid Marietta of all Jews by the above date. You can heed this warning or stand the punishment the committee may see fit to deal out to you.

A mob assembled in downtown Atlanta and marched to the governor's mansion. They threw rocks and bottles at the state militia troops who stood guard with bayonets uncovered. After a week of violent demonstrations, Gov. Slaton attended the inauguration of his successor, Nathaniel Harris, and then left the state.

In the Milledgeville Prison, a fellow inmate slashed Leo Frank's throat. Frank survived, telling his doctor, "I am going to live. I must live. I must vindicate myself."

A month later, 25 prominent citizens of Marietta forced their way into the prison before midnight. They called themselves the Knights of Mary Phagan. They handcuffed the warden and the superintendent and easily subdued the two guards. Within five minutes they had removed Leo Frank from his hospital room.

"Don't bother with the clothes," they told him. "Come just as you are."

The line of cars sped through the dark countryside. Frank remained calm as his captors tried to force a confession. The sound of his voice as he answered them caused a couple of the men to wonder if he really was guilty after all.

They stopped their car to confer with the others. Frank spoke again, and afterward all

> "I would rather be the widow of a brave and honorable man than the wife of a coward."

but four of the men were willing to take him back to the prison. But the posses were out, someone objected. They agreed it was too late to change their minds.

They took him to a big oak tree. They tied a Manila rope expertly into a hangman's coil.

"Mr. Frank, we are now going to do what the law said to do," the leader said. "Hang you by the neck until you are dead."

Frank asked that his wedding band be removed and returned to his wife. The men obliged him. Then they tossed the rope over a limb, placed the noose around Frank's neck and lifted him onto a table.

Toward morning, a crowd of Marietta residents gathered to celebrate at the tree where the body hung. Some cut snippets of the rope with their pocket knives or tore shreds from Leo Frank's nightshirt as souvenirs. ◆

Right. Georgia merchants sold postcard photographs of the Leo Frank lynching.

Anti-Semitism in History

Almost everywhere Jewish people have lived in the world, they have suffered from anti-Semitism. (The Jews belong to a population group known as the Semites. Arabs are Semites, too, but the term anti-Semitic usually means "anti-Jewish.") In ancient times, hatred of the Jews was mainly an expression of religious intolerance. The Greeks and Romans, who worshipped numerous gods and goddesses, ridiculed Jewish monotheism. For centuries, many Christians blamed Jews for the death of Jesus, and some people continue to justify anti-Semitism on those grounds.

During the Middle Ages, gruesome legends were created to portray Jews as evil. Most cities of Europe placed severe restrictions on where Jews could live. Our modern word for a minority neighborhood comes from the old Jewish section of Venice — the Ghetto. In some places, every Jew was required to wear a yellow ID badge.

Expressions of prejudice toward Jews over the centuries have ranged from persecution to expulsion to slaughter. In 18th-century Europe, a new emphasis on religious freedom temporarily broke the pattern. But the rise of nationalism in the 19th century gave anti-Semitism a new foundation: racial pride.

This was the idea that brought Adolf Hitler to power in Germany in the early

1930s. Before World War II toppled Hitler's government, his Nazi Party had murdered some six million Jews.

A number of public figures in U.S. history have practiced or preached forms of anti-Semitism. During the Civil War, Gen. Ulysses S. Grant ordered all Jewish merchants to leave his military district on the grounds that they had been trading illegally in cotton. It apparently didn't matter to Grant that some of his own relatives (and many other non-Jews) had been doing the same thing.

Automotive giant Henry Ford published books and articles in the 1920s that accused Jews of plotting to take over the world. In his view, both the Civil War and Abraham Lincoln's assassination had resulted from Jewish conspiracies.

An American Catholic priest, Father Charles Coughlin, rose to prominence in the 1930s with a radio program and magazine promoting anti-Semitic ideas. Ironically, one thing that prevented Coughlin from gaining wider influence was the fact that many of his listeners and readers were also anti-Catholic.

More recently, Nation of Islam leader Louis Farrakhan has charged that Jews ran the slave trade and continue to exploit African Americans economically. Farrakhan's speeches echo many of the oldest myths of anti-Semitism.

While such open expressions of hatred toward Jews are rare in the United States, hidden prejudices are common, even in "civilized" circles of society and government. Many white Protestant country clubs traditionally excluded Jews from membership. Similarly, the "old-boy" networks of the foreign service and certain elite universities once used quotas and other restrictions to limit Jewish admission. While most such policies are now illegal, patterns of preference in some institutions remain.

In the early 1980s, the rise of the neo-Nazi Skinhead movement brought anti-Semitism in the U.S. to a new level of violence. Incidents of personal harassment and assaults against Jews by white supremacist youths increased dramatically during that decade,

along with vandalism of synagogues and Jewish cemeteries.

Like most white supremacist groups, Skinheads combine hatred of Jews with a general intolerance toward all minorities. Their devotion to "white power" has often allied them with older white supremacists, who welcome a new generation willing to fight the battles of hate.

Untamed Border

Memoirs, novels and movies have depicted the Mexican border "bandit wars" of the early 20th century in such a romantic light that many innocent casualties of the conflict have been forgotten. For decades, the predominant American stereotype of the Mexican was a bandoleered bandito with a long mustache and an evil grin. Conversely, the white-hatted Texas Ranger has ridden high through the literature of the West, his gleaming twin six-shooters always at the ready.

The mythology of border outlaws and lawmen hides thousands of unknown victims behind these cartoon images. When the famous 19th-century Texas gunman King Fisher was asked how many notches he sported on his gun, he answered, "Thirty-seven — not counting Mexicans."

ON CHRISTMAS DAY 1917, bandits from Mexico raided L. C. Brite's ranch in Presidio County, Texas, killing two Mexican laborers and an Anglo stage driver, stealing horses and robbing the ranch store. U.S. soldiers stationed nearby followed the bandits back into Mexico.

Exactly a month later, on the night of January 25, 1918, an armed and mounted posse of Anglos consisting of Texas Rangers and ranch owners converged on the Mexican settlement of El Porvenir in Presidio County.

Soldiers who showed them the way were told that the men had come to arrest suspects in the Brite ranch raid. The Rangers — some wearing masks — ordered all residents out of their homes. They took three men into the nearby mountains and held them for two days under a threat of death before letting them go.

On the third night, January 28, the posse returned to El Porvenir around 2 a.m. and conducted another round-up. This time, they selected 15 men and boys, marched them at gunpoint several hundred yards away from the

houses, and, without a word, shot each one in the head. Searchers found no items belonging to the Brite ranch in any of the El Porvenir homes.

The surviving members of the community moved as quickly as they could to Mexico, taking with them the 15 corpses but leaving behind their cows and goats, their well-stocked grain bins and their fields newly sown with wheat. No one was ever punished for the murders.

For more than a century in the back country and scattered towns of the Rio Grande Valley, the Texas Rangers were a law unto themselves. The Ranger force originated in 1821 as a band of Indian fighters hired by Stephen Austin to protect the first Anglo, or white, settlers entering the Mexican territory of Texas. "Protection" often meant helping the settlers seize Indian land.

> *Tejanos suspected of crimes were hanged or shot without trial.*

As Indian resistance subsided, the Rangers turned to harassing the Tejanos, or Texas Mexicans, whose farms and rangeland the Anglos also coveted. Organized officially in 1835, the Rangers served as a paramilitary police force in the short-lived Texas Republic (1836-45) and conducted raids across the border during the Mexican War (1846-48).

Mexicans living north of the Rio Grande became U.S. citizens when Texas attained statehood in 1845, yet the Rangers systematically denied them justice. Tejanos suspected of crimes were hanged or shot without trial. A Mexican's word was considered worthless in most courts of law. By the early 20th century, the Rangers' reputation for racist violence and intimidation brought comparisons with the Ku Klux Klan, although at least one famous Ranger, Jesús Sandoval, was himself Mexican.

Ranger terrorism increased sharply after 1910, as the Mexican Revolution (1910-20) spawned confusion all along the border.

Right. Raids on Texas herds by Mexican bandits brought financial hardship to Anglo ranchers and increased intolerance toward Tejanos.

Opposite page. Rangers at Ysleta, Texas, display a Mexican prisoner in 1894.

Followers of guerrilla leader Pancho Villa crossed back and forth, attacking Americans to create havoc for the Mexican president. Mexican ranchers, afraid that civil war would wreck the national economy, herded their cattle north across the Rio Grande to take advantage of America's wartime demand for beef. The abandoned Mexican range land sprouted a thick coat of grass, and enterprising outlaws soon recognized its potential: They ventured north and rounded up American-owned livestock to drive south and fatten up for sale in Mexico.

The losses to the Texas economy were enormous, and the Mexican outlaws made little distinction between Anglo and Tejano victims. In keeping with their history, however, the Rangers openly favored Anglo interests. Even law-abiding Tejanos became the objects of suspicion and abuse. In some counties, Rangers confiscated the firearms of Tejano citizens, including officers of the law. Without guns for protection, many Mexican Americans lost all their farm animals to thieves and coyotes.

The onset of World War I in 1914 made the border situation even more explosive. As American troops shipped off to Europe to fight the Germans, Texas authorities feared that Mexican Americans eligible for the draft were evading military service by heading south. Furthermore, rumors alleged that Germany was arming Mexicans and using Mexican agents to distribute propaganda in Texas in order to undermine the U.S. war effort.

In June 1916, Pres. Woodrow Wilson responded to the mounting crisis by mobilizing some 100,000 National Guardsmen from Texas, New Mexico and Arizona to patrol the border. By the following year, 35,000 U.S. Army troops were stationed there as well. For many Anglos in South Texas, the triple threat of banditry, draft evasion and espionage justified an "open season" on Mexicans. Up and down the valley, whole villages were raided and their inhabitants driven across the river or killed. The El Porvenir round-up was a typical example.

A "black list" kept by the Rangers during this period contained the names of Mexicans targeted for elimination. Any Tejano who appeared on the list had two choices: He could cross the Rio Grande and take refuge in Mexico, or he could wait for someone to discover his corpse on the U.S. side. It didn't take much to qualify for black-listing. A Mexican's name could be added by any man of standing — "or even half-way standing," as one white lawyer explained.

As the anti-Mexican climate intensified, the Rangers revived the old frontier policy of "Shoot first, ask questions later," which resulted in a high toll on innocent lives. Historians estimate that more than 500 Tejanos were summarily executed by the Rangers during the "bandit wars" of the 1910s and '20s. Many of these victims were described by their families and communities as having "evaporated" without a trace.

As it had for decades, violence against Mexican Americans by Rangers during this era generally went unchecked by local governments or law enforcement agencies. The most avid Mexican-haters on the force flouted all regard for arrest warrants, trial by jury and other legal rights.

DOCUMENT

"The Government of a white race"

In 1848, Sen. John C. Calhoun of South Carolina argued before the U.S. Senate against annexing any more of Mexico.

We have never dreamt of incorporating into our Union any but the Caucasian race — the free white race. To incorporate Mexico, would be the very first instance of the kind of incorporating an Indian race; for more than half of the Mexicans are Indians, and the other is composed chiefly of mixed tribes. I protest against such a union as that! Ours, sir, is the Government of a white race. The greatest misfortunes of Spanish America are to be traced to the fatal error of placing these colored races on an equality with the white race. That error destroyed the social arrangement which formed the basis of society. ...

Are we to overlook this fact? Are we to associate with ourselves as equals, companions, and fellow-citizens, the Indians and mixed race of Mexico? Sir, I should consider such a thing as fatal to our institutions.

On September 3, 1918, Jesús Villareal of Copita, Texas, agreed to take two teenage sons of a friend along with him on a trip to Rio Grande City, on the north bank of the river. The two boys intended to buy some goats from a man near there. Outside of Rio Grande City, just after midnight, a Texas Ranger stepped out onto the road in front of Jesús' car.

The Ranger asked Jesús to take him a mile or so to where he had left his own car when the radiator ran dry. Jesús complied, and when he reached the parked vehicle he saw three more Rangers. Two of them took the boys out of Jesús' car and led them away. The other two Rangers told Jesús he was under arrest.

Out of the glare of the headlights, and out of earshot from Jesús, the Rangers asked the boys where they were going. Eulalio Benavides, age 18, told them about the goats. One of the

IN CONTEXT

The Second Burial of Felix Longoria

U nder the "shoot first" rule of the Texas Rangers, hatred toward Tejanos took a dramatic and deadly form. For the thousands of Mexican Americans who avoided Ranger bullets, the prejudice of Anglos was a quiet, routine fact of life. 'No Mexicans,' declared signs in shop windows. Tejano tax dollars supported 'White Only' swimming pools. Job discrimination closed the doors of economic opportunity.

In many Texas counties, Tejano children attended separate, inferior schools. As the Longoria family of Three Rivers discovered, the barriers confronting Mexican Americans extended even beyond death.

For the first 10 years of its existence, Three Rivers had one cemetery. Anglo and Mexican residents buried their dead in the same ground. After a while, this "togetherness" began to make some of the Anglos uncomfortable. They felt that the cemetery should more closely resemble the rest of Three Rivers, with its Anglo neighborhoods and separate "Mexican Town." In 1924, a committee of Anglos told Guadalupe Longoria that the time had come to establish a graveyard for his people. A new area was set aside next to the old one, and someone strung up a length of barbed wire in between.

At the age of five, Guadalupe's son Felix was too young to understand the cemetery matter, but as he grew older he learned about the other boundaries that defined his world. It wasn't until he joined the Army in 1945 that Felix experienced the full equality of his citizenship. Unlike their African American counterparts, Mexican American servicemen were not segregated from the majority.

On June 16, 1945, while scouting for enemy positions in a jungle of the Philippines, Felix Longoria was struck by a Japanese sniper's bullet and killed instantly. His comrades buried him in a military cemetery on Luzon Island. Less than three months later, Japan surrendered and the war was over.

Back in Texas and across the Southwest, Mexican American veterans returned to their old

Rangers said that Eulalio was lying, that he and his brother were planning to cross the river to avoid the draft. The Ranger slapped Eulalio and struck him in the head with a pistol.

"Say that you are going across," the Ranger demanded, taking hold of Eulalio's throat and pressing the pistol to his chest. "If you don't say you are going to the other side, I'll kill you."

Eulalio nodded his head. The Rangers took the boys back to where Jesús was being held.

They told Jesús that the boys had accused him of contracting to deliver them into Mexican territory. When he protested, explaining about the goats, two of the Rangers escorted Jesús into the darkness. They told him to lie down, face-up. One of them sat on Jesús' stomach and ordered him to admit his real intentions. "If you don't," they said, "we'll kill you."

"You can do what you please," said Jesús. "I've told you the truth."

walks of life with a new sense of both ethnic and national pride. But they quickly discovered that the old obstacles remained. In March 1948, a group of Mexican Americans in Corpus Christi established the American GI Forum to monitor and advocate the equal distribution of veterans' benefits.

Later that same year, military authorities notified Beatrice Longoria that her husband's body was being transported home for reburial. She arranged to have his wake held at the local mortuary rather than in her own living room, as was the Mexican custom.

While Felix's remains were en route, the owner of Rice Funeral Home told Beatrice that she would have to change her plans. The establishment couldn't provide its chapel service for the Longorias after all, he said, "because the whites would not like it."

At her sister's urging, Beatrice sent word of the matter to Dr. Hector Garcia, founder of the GI Forum, who contacted local, state and federal officials. Newspapers across the country picked up the story. During a protest meeting at Three Rivers, a courier delivered a telegram from U.S. Sen. Lyndon Johnson of Texas, which read in part: "I have today made arrangements to have Felix Longoria reburied with full military honors in Arlington National Cemetery … where the hon-

Felix Longoria

ored dead of our nation's wars rest."

The funeral took place on Feb. 16, 1949, as a grey drizzle shrouded the gentle slopes of Arlington. Felix's whole family was there. Sen. Johnson and his wife came to pay their respects. Mexican diplomats brought flowers in tribute from their country.

For some Texas Anglos, the military funeral of Felix Longoria opened a wound rather than healed one: In the national headlines, Three Rivers had been disgraced.

A committee appointed by the state legislature held hearings at Three Rivers on the discrimination charges. Witnesses testified for both sides, but the atmosphere was decidedly anti-Mexican. Anglo observers openly used ethnic slurs. The Longoria family, Dr. Garcia and others received anonymous death threats by mail and by phone.

The committee initially concluded that no racial discrimination had occurred against Beatrice Longoria, but members later called the report into question and it was withdrawn. The Felix Longoria case brought the American GI Forum to national prominence. The group would eventually become the nation's largest organization of Mexican Americans.

"Shooting Out the Lights"

Texas Ranger N. A. Jennings published a memoir of his years in the Ranger service. The following excerpt describes a "raid" across the border to the Mexican town of Matamoras in 1875.

We paid frequent visits to Matamoras after nightfall. We went there for two reasons: to have fun, and to carry out a set policy of terrorizing the Mexicans at every opportunity.

Half a dozen of the boys would leave camp after dark and make their way over the river to Matamoras by way of the ferry. If we could find a fandango, or Mexican dance, going on, we would enter the dancing-hall and break up the festivities by shooting out the lights. This would naturally result in much confusion and, added to the reports of our revolvers, would be the shrill screaming of women and cursing of angry Mexicans. Soldiers would come running from all directions. We would then fire a few more shots in the air and make off for the ferry, as fast as we could go.

When we reached Brownsville, we would hunt another fandango — there were always some of these dances going on every night — and proceed, as in Matamoras, to break it up.

Both Rangers clutched Jesús — one by the throat, the other over the nose and mouth. They choked him until he almost passed out. After they finally let go and told him to speak, he couldn't catch his breath.

"The boys are lying," Jesús said at last.

They repeated the threat. Jesús was insistent. One of the Rangers then jammed the barrel of his pistol into Jesús' mouth. "What do you say?" the Ranger taunted. "Is it so, what the boys say, or not?"

The Ranger removed the pistol, and Jesús again said, "No." Again he felt the cold gun-barrel grinding against his teeth.

The other Ranger pulled out a knife, but his partner told him to wait until Jesús was dead. Then they could put the knife in his hand and claim that he had jumped them.

But they changed their minds. After the interrogation, the Rangers drove Jesús and his companions to a nearby U.S. Army camp and put them in the guardhouse to await trial in Federal Court at Brownsville, where the three were found innocent of charges and released. By Ranger standards, Jesús Villareal had gotten off easy.

Reports of Ranger abuses prompted

Texas state legislator J. T. Canales, a Tejano from Brownsville, to sponsor a legislative investigation in 1919. The hearings produced testimony from both Anglo and Mexican witnesses of verbal abuse, torture and murder of Mexican Americans by Texas Rangers.

As a result of the Canales investigation, the legislature voted to reduce the Ranger force and to make it easier for citizens to lodge complaints against individual Rangers. These institutional reforms acknowledged a legacy of injustice in Texas law enforcement, but they did not bring an end to anti-Tejano violence. The old hatreds along the border still burned, and whites who killed Tejanos continued to go free.

Among the forgotten victims was Bernadino Campos. Campos worked for J. Adams on the Keystone ranch near Pearsall, in Frio County. On the morning of May 24, 1920, Adams complained that Campos wasn't doing his job. Campos suggested that if Adams was not satisfied, then Campos would terminate his contract and look for work somewhere else. Adams agreed and went to his house to get the money to pay Campos off.

When Adams returned on horseback, he approached Campos and, in the presence of two witnesses, shot at him with a pistol. Campos wasn't hit. He managed to grab the horse's bridle and pick up a stone. But as Campos tried to defend himself, Adams fired twice more and killed him.

Despite the eyewitnesses and a recommendation of the Public Minister that he be imprisoned, Adams' political and financial connections helped him win acquittal. The court's message was clear: Though a Tejano spent his life under the watchful eyes of Anglos, he was beneath all notice in death. ◆

Opposite page. Following a bandit raid near Norias, Texas, in 1915, postcards depicting Rangers and dead Mexicans were sold by the thousands.

Left. Outward signs and invisible barriers deprived Mexican Americans of their civil rights.

IN CONTEXT

The Zoot-Suit Riots

World War II is often credited with pulling the country together. As their compatriots defended democracy abroad, however, some Americans met hostile forces on the home front.

Los Angeles in the 1940s was swamped with GIs. The entertainment capital drew thousands of servicemen on leave from nearby bases and training centers.

As it does today, the civilian population of L.A. then included a large Mexican American, or Chicano, minority. Many

of the Anglo servicemen in town came from areas of the country where there weren't a lot of Chicanos. Here they heard stories about Chicano youth gangs and about how to pick up Chicanas, or Mexican girls.

Lately, a Chicano teenage fashion trend called the zoot suit — modeled on flashy mobster attire — had been widely ridiculed in the Anglo press. Visiting servicemen joined in harassing the strutting and posing "zoot-suiters." In the spring and summer of 1943, tension between GIs and young Mexican American males turned violent.

In Oakland and Venice, Calif., sailors and marines "raided" Chicano gatherings and attacked the zoot-suiters, stripping them of their clothes. On June 3 in Los Angeles, a reported dispute over Chicanas set off a military riot. For five straight nights, Anglos in uniform stormed the streets. They dragged zoot-suiters out of bars and nabbed them in movie theaters by turning the lights on.

What started as an assault on Mexican Americans quickly expanded to include blacks and Filipinos. Each night, police officers waited until the GIs had left and then swooped in to

arrest the victims of the violence.

Fearing mutiny, military officials declared the downtown district off limits to military personnel. The measure restored order, but real peace would be harder to achieve. In a national newspaper column, First Lady Eleanor Roosevelt blamed the riots on "long-standing discrimination against the Mexicans in the Southwest."

A rebuttal by the *Los Angeles Times* ended with the statement "We like Mexicans and think they like us." This wording makes clear that, as far as official Los Angeles was concerned, Mexican Americans were still "them."

A Town Called Rosewood

The end of World War I marked the beginning of a turbulent period for race relations in America. The wartime economy had drawn a wave of African American workers from the South into Northern cities. Returning veterans found jobs scarce as factories scaled back or closed altogether. Economic hardship aggravated old prejudices. The Ku Klux Klan experienced a nationwide revival, and in most major U.S. cities groups of angry whites rioted through African American neighborhoods.

In the rural South, lynch mobs stepped up their reign of terror over the black population. By the rules of "Judge Lynch," any perceived offense against a white person — particularly a white woman — was punishable by death. Whistling at a schoolgirl could get a black man hanged. The residents of one Florida hamlet learned how far this jurisdiction of hate extended.

TODAY THE WOODS AND SWAMPS of Levy County in north central Florida are mostly uninhabited, but in the latter half of the 19th century and early part of the 20th, they were dotted with thriving villages whose citizens made their living off the region's natural wealth. Timber companies chopped down red cedar for manufacturing pencils; turpentine stills boiled and distilled pine sap; women wove the leaves of the spiky palmetto into brooms and brushes; men hunted and trapped the abundant wildlife.

There are few reminders in the woods today of this enterprising era. The tracks of the railroads that once connected the villages have been lifted for scrap, and the overgrown rail embankments now pass through mile after mile of unvarying pine forest. The towns that flourished there, towns like Rosewood, Sumner and Wylly, survive only as names on old train schedules and in the memories of a few elderly men and women.

It is an obscure moment in Florida's history, and it might have been forgotten — except

that something happened in these woods, something so awful that decades later some people can hardly bring themselves to speak about it.

It all began on January 1, 1923, a day that survivors and eyewitnesses would remember as bitterly cold. On that morning, a young, married white woman named Fannie Taylor emerged from her home in Sumner in extreme shock. Her husband had left early for work at the town's lumber mill. In his absence, she said, a stranger, a black man, had come into her house and assaulted her. Though she was not badly injured physically, Fannie Taylor lapsed into unconsciousness for several hours soon after describing the attack.

The Levy County Sheriff, Robert Elias Walker, quickly assembled a posse and deputized several men to help search for Taylor's assailant. They were joined by a large and growing number of white men from the area, who were outraged at this violation of Southern white womanhood.

"This crowd wants blood," warned Sheriff Walker, "and they [are] going to have blood." Together, the men followed a pack of hounds into the neighboring town of Rosewood, looking for the man they suspected of the assault: a prisoner named Jesse Hunter, who had escaped from a nearby chain gang where he was serving time for carrying a concealed weapon.

In the early 1920s, Rosewood was a solid, largely African American community of between 100 and 200 people. It boasted three churches, a train station, two general stores, a Masonic hall and a one-room schoolhouse. It

> *"This crowd wants blood," warned Sheriff Walker, "and they [are] going to have blood."*

was, as a white resident of Levy County would later characterize it, a "good community," whose "people had nice homes and were law-abiding and took care of themselves."

The bloodhounds led the posse to the home of a blacksmith named Sam Carter. Carter, a 45-year-old African American, had had a brush with the law once before. In 1920, he was accused of assaulting a police officer but was set free when the grand jury failed to indict him. Questioned by the posse, Carter admitted that he had driven the suspect away in his horse and wagon. He took the men to the spot where, he claimed, he had dropped the man off. But the hounds weren't able to pick up the fugitive's scent. Carter insisted that this was the spot, but the posse, thinking they had been duped, tortured Carter, then hanged and shot him. His corpse was left lying in the road where it was discovered the next morning.

For the next two days, the white mob combed the area, looking for Jesse Hunter. During that time, they harassed, intimidated and threatened to lynch blacks that they came upon. They dragged one young black man, Aaron Carrier, whom they suspected of helping the fugitive escape, from his sickbed to a stand of pine trees and would have hanged him if a white mill supervisor named W.H. Pillsbury had not intervened. Twice, the posse warned Sylvester Carrier, another resident of Rosewood, that he had better be careful about what he said and about his attitude around whites. Some even told him he should leave town.

Sylvester Carrier was not one to take these threats submissively. A proud, strong man who was active in the African Methodist Episcopal Church, Carrier taught music, was a crack shot and hunted for his livelihood. One of the most respected men in Rosewood, he was also married to a woman who was described as extraordinarily beautiful.

On January 4, the mob heard rumors that some African Americans, including Sylvester Carrier, had barricaded themselves inside a two-story house in Rosewood owned by Sylvester's mother, Sarah Carrier. The mob surrounded the house, and two of the men, who were acquainted with the Carrier family, approached the front door. Accounts differ as

to whether the men tried to force their way in, but in any case they didn't get far: A round of gunfire from inside the house killed them both on the porch.

Now the mob unleashed their fury. They poured volley after volley of lead into the house, and as day turned to a bright, moonlit night, the siege and the fusillade continued. At 2:30 in the morning, a solitary white man made his way toward the house across the open field separating the two armed camps. As he tried to enter the house through a darkened window, he was shot in the head. The next day the local newspapers reported that a man was dying of a gunshot wound but never gave his name. The man's identity remains a mystery to this day.

Finally, at about 4 a.m., the whites ran low on ammunition and left to replenish their supply. The surviving blacks took advantage of the lull in the fighting to flee. At dawn, when the whites returned, they retrieved their two dead from the front porch and discovered in the now-quiet house the lifeless bodies of Sarah and Sylvester Carrier, killed in the midnight siege.

That the blacks had escaped — with the exception of the two Carriers — was for many whites the final insult. They went on a rampage, setting fire to five houses and a church in the immediate vicinity. Most of the black residents of the area had already fled into the

Opposite page, above. Turpentine production was a major industry in the pine forests around Rosewood.

Opposite page, below. In late December 1923, one Florida landowner capitalized on African Americans' desire for self-determination.

Above. After the violence ended, the survivors of the Rosewood riot had no homes to return to.

woods, but one woman, Lexie Gordon, had hidden under her house during the night. As it went up in flames, she ran toward a clump of bushes and was shot in the back.

Twenty miles from Rosewood, Mingo Williams, nicknamed "Lord God," was shot through the jaw by whites who had been drinking. The posse had graduated from being a lynch mob, which at least pretended to identify the guilty parties before murdering them, to being "nigger hunters." On a "nigger hunt," any and all blacks became targets. Williams, a 50-year-old turpentine worker, had nothing to do with Rosewood or the events there. His only crime was that he was a black man who happened to be in the wrong place at the wrong time.

Nearly all the African American men and women who remember Rosewood today were children at the time of these events. What they remember most vividly is being awakened at night and taken, while still in their nightclothes, into the overgrown hammocks. Cold and hungry, they endured several days in the swampy woods, not daring to light much of a fire for fear of attracting the mob. "It was cold, man, it was cold," one survivor testified years later. "Jesus, I will never forget that day."

On Saturday morning, January 6, James Carrier, Sylvester's brother, turned himself over to the white superintendent of the Sumner lumber mill for protection. W.H. Pillsbury, the mill superintendent, had tried to protect Sylvester earlier in the week, and now he tried to help James, locking him in one of

IN CONTEXT

Race Riots

Today, when we hear the term "race riot" we are apt to think of the burning and looting that has occurred in poor, primarily black urban areas since the 1960s — of Watts, for example, a neighborhood in Los Angeles where anger about the conditions of ghetto life exploded in 1965, leading to 34 deaths in six days. Or we think of South Central Los Angeles in 1992, where violence erupted after a jury found white policemen not guilty of beating a black motorist named Rodney King, despite a videotape that clearly showed them clubbing and kicking King. The riot that followed that verdict left at least 45 people dead and caused an estimated $1 billion in damages.

Yet for many decades, the instigators and

participants in race riots were usually white, not black, and the purpose of the rioting was to assert white domination rather than to express black anger and frustration. During Reconstruction and for a while thereafter, race riots often occurred during elections, as white mobs sought to intimidate the newly enfranchised black voters and to regain power from politicians who would give blacks an equal opportunity in post-Civil War society. Riots in Memphis, Tenn.; New Orleans, La.; Charleston, S.C.; and Eufaula, Ala., led to dozens of African American deaths.

Prior to the 1898 election in Wilmington, N.C., whites took to wearing red shirts to symbolize their willingness to resort to the Winchester rifle and "a baptism of blood" to regain power. They would teach the "Southern Negroes that they cannot rule over the property and the destinies of the superior race," the

Rosewood's dozen remaining houses. But somehow James's whereabouts were discovered later that day. James was driven to the black cemetery, and there, beside the newly dug graves of his mother and brother, he was interrogated and tortured. When he refused to give up the names of the people who had joined him and his brother in the shoot-out, he was riddled with bullets and left to bleed to death.

The whites returned to Rosewood and torched the remaining houses, the churches, the school, the black-owned general store and the Masonic Lodge. "Masses of twisted steel were all that remained of furniture formerly in the Negro homes, [and] several charred bodies of dogs,

and firearms left in the hasty retreat, bore evidence to the mob's fury," the *Gainesville Daily Sun* reported at the time.

Not all the whites in the area joined the mob. One who refused out of conscience to help the vigilantes said that he did not want to "have his hands wet with blood." Others did their best to prevent the violence from spreading. Pillsbury maintained strict discipline at the mill. He established a curfew, segregated the black workers into a special section of the mill and warned whites that anyone who crossed the line into that section would be shot.

Other whites tried to help. John Wright, who owned a general store in Rosewood and lived in a two-story white frame house near the railroad depot, was

Washington Post editorialized, commending the Red Shirts.

Although white supremacists gave ample notice of their willingness to resort to violence, little effort was made to protect African Americans, and as many as 25 lost their lives in the weeks leading up to the election. The bigots won the election handily, despite spirited opposition from black political leaders and clergymen.

By the early part of the 20th century, race riots in New York City, Atlanta, Springfield (home of Abraham Lincoln), Houston and East St. Louis had left scores of blacks dead. Almost invariably, white authorities did little or nothing to protect African Americans, while clamping down hard on those who exercised the right of self-defense.

There were 27 separate race riots and countless lesser acts of racial violence in 1919 alone, including the following:

• In Texas, one man was killed and an African American school principal was publicly flogged after a local newspaper article condemned lynching.

• In Chicago, a race riot erupted after an African American youth was stoned while

swimming at an all-white beach, resulting in his death by drowning. Thirty-eight people were killed in two weeks of sustained violence, and 1,000 black families were left homeless.

• In Georgia, a black World War I veteran was beaten to death for wearing his uniform in public. The mob ignored the man's protests that he had no other clothes.

• In Knoxville, Tenn., six persons were killed and 20 injured after unsuccessful attempts to lynch a black prisoner charged with killing a white woman. Afterwards, U.S. troops shot up a black neighborhood on the basis of false rumors that blacks had killed two white men.

• In Louisiana, an illiterate black man suspected of writing an insulting note to a white woman escaped lynch mobs twice before he was finally shot to death.

• In Arkansas, a riot by white racists left up to 200 blacks dead. The violence resulted in 79 murder indictments — all against blacks. Twelve were convicted and sentenced to die before their convictions were overturned on appeal.

FIRST PERSON

Tulsa Riot, 1921

More than 70 years after the event, Dr. Hobart Jarrett recounted the experience of being driven from his family home. In 1960, as a professor in Greensboro, N.C., Dr. Jarrett became the principal spokesperson for African Americans during the sit-in movement that opened local lunch counters to black patrons.

I remember how we found out that there was going to be a riot. I was six years old. My mother and father were taking me several blocks up the street to a church, where I was to recite a poem. As we were going south, we kept meeting people heading north, the direction from which we had come. My father stopped two men, asking what all the commotion was about. They said the whites were going to take a black man out of the jail.

My father, mother and I turned and went back home. The next morning, as I can recall, we all — uncles, nephews, cousins, grandmother, great-grandmother — headed out of town by truck. It was remarkable to me later on to realize that my grandfather — whom I called Uncle Bill — did not run with us. He stayed at home. I have heard all my life that Uncle Bill stayed there

(Continued on page 90)

(Continued from page 89)

Tulsa Riot, 1921

with his rifle on his porch. Our home and his home were not burned because he was there.

He did not keep the rioters from *entering* the homes. When we got back, everything was in disorder. Clothing was scattered. I had a Little Boy Blue bank sitting on the piano. I had saved 13 dollars. The money and bank were not taken by the looters. That became my father's capital — all the money he had left.

Our grocery store was burned to the ground. It was on the south side of the Negro section of town. He had kept his money in the safe. That was all gone.

I remember that at some point we stayed on somebody's farm. Some black person's farm. When we got back to Tulsa after two days, we were herded into the fairgrounds, and I recall that I was very, very hungry, and there was a soup-line — a line of blacks — for beans. They were in a cauldron. I ate a lot of beans. I also recall that for years thereafter, I couldn't eat any dried beans at all.

A relative — a dear, dear cousin of mine from Texas — was visiting with my grandmother at that unfortunate time. He said that the rioters had urinated on the floor in my grandmother's home and on her Victrola. I remember this because this was the first time I heard the word 'urinated.'

fond of the neighborhood children and used to give them free candy and cookies whenever they came into his store. He hid several families in his house and others under a wooden boardwalk connecting his store to the train depot. Two brothers who worked as railroad conductors, William and John Bryce, brought a train into the Rosewood depot and took dozens of women and children to safety.

Jesse Hunter, the suspected assailant of Fannie Taylor, was never found. Eventually, the mob gave up and went about their daily lives. Yet the black town of Rosewood was reduced to rubble and abandoned.

"We lost everything," said one survivor. Homes, possessions, community: Nothing remained.

No one knows for sure how many people ultimately died in that week-long rampage. The newspapers named eight dead, but rumors of mass graves lingered in Levy County for decades. Many today still believe there are dozens of others who probably lost their lives.

Because the community dispersed after the riots, the survivors could never be certain whether their neighbors and friends had escaped or perished in the swamps. Other, more gruesome, rumors tell of body parts preserved in vinegar jars as mementos of the "hunt."

But perhaps the most intriguing rumor

doesn't concern the number of dead or the fate of their bodies but the identity of Fannie Taylor's assailant. African American survivors and the children of survivors are adamant on one point: Taylor's assailant was not a strange black man but her white lover.

According to this version of events, the lovers had quarreled and he had beaten her. To save her reputation, Fannie Taylor invented the story of the black man. Her lover, meanwhile, fled to Rosewood and sought refuge with Sam Carter because Carter, like himself, was a member of the Masonic Order, a secret society whose members pledged themselves to brotherhood, charity and mutual aid. Carter had concealed the identity of the suspect in order to protect his fellow Mason and had paid for his loyalty with his life.

The visitor to Rosewood today will see a green town marker on Route 24, about 40 miles west of Gainesville. John Wright's home is still standing, and a walk through the woods eventually reveals a cluster of crumbled headstones overgrown with weeds. Aside from the highway marker, there is nothing else to indicate that there was once a town called Rosewood. ◆

IN CONTEXT

Rosewood Revisited

On April 8, 1994, 18 well-dressed African Americans, most of them elderly and frail, lined the spectators' gallery at the Florida House of Representatives in Tallahassee. Survivors of the Rosewood massacre, or children of survivors, they were there to witness an extraordinary moment in American history.

On that day, the Florida state legislature was to debate a reparations bill that would grant up to $150,000 compensation to each of the survivors and set aside a college fund for their descendants. If the bill passed, it would mark the first time in history that African Americans would be compensated for crimes committed against them as a result of their race.

Opposition to the claims bill was fierce. The Ku Klux Klan held rallies in Levy County protesting the bill. Many state senators and representatives also opposed it, as did a large number of ordinary white Floridians. Why hold today's taxpayers responsible for the crimes of an earlier era? they asked. Wasn't the legislature setting a dangerous precedent? Weren't there dozens, perhaps even hundreds, of similar events in Florida's history? There were 47 lynchings in Florida from 1912 to 1927 alone. What made Rosewood special?

Fortunately, the survivors had powerful friends on their side. The largest law firm in the state was representing them on a pro bono, or free, basis. Lawyers working on the case modeled their claims bill on the bill passed by the United States Congress granting compensation to Japanese Americans who had been unconstitutionally interned during World War II *(see p. 99)*. And Florida Gov. Lawton Chiles had announced he was strongly in favor of the compensation package.

Still, it was a tough fight. The state senate committee responsible for claims passed the bill by a three-vote margin. When it came to the final vote in Florida's House of Representatives, supporters urged the legislators, as one of the sponsors said, to "let conscience be your guide." Rosewood was special, they said, not only because eight people lost their lives, but because an entire town was eliminated, its inhabitants dispersed. The violence had gone on for a week, and while Rosewood burned, the governor had gone hunting.

Finally, the bill came to a vote, and when the votes were tallied, the bill had passed 71 to 40. While the Rosewood survivors in the spectators' balcony wept in gratitude, the legislators rose to their feet to applaud them — the men and women who had waited so long and so patiently to see justice served.

Home Was a Horse Stall

On Dec. 7, 1941, Japan's attack on the U.S. naval station at Pearl Harbor, Hawaii, thrust the United States into World War II and changed the life of every American. Thousands of young men were drafted into the Army and sent halfway around the globe to risk their lives in battle. The long, lean years of the Depression abruptly ended as American industry geared up for wartime. In factories and businesses and government bureaus, women played a more prominent role in the national work force than ever before.

Both the news and entertainment media of the era depicted a nation rallying to the defense of freedom. But one group of Americans faced a struggle all its own. For Americans of Japanese descent, the experience of the war years gave the word "freedom" a whole new meaning.

YUMI ISHIMARU WAS USED TO picking up and moving on. In 1905, at the age of 20, she left Yamaguchi, Japan, for San Francisco to marry a man she had only seen in a picture. After being detained with other "picture brides" for medical tests at Angel Island, Yumi reached the mainland, met Masajiro Kataoka, and found him shorter than she had expected.

Masajiro, also from Yamaguchi, operated a restaurant off Fillmore Street. After they were married, Yumi went to work as a house-keeper for an American family. Before long, she was expecting her first child. The Kataokas' prospects looked good. But the great earthquake of April 1906 destroyed Masajiro's restaurant and left the young couple homeless. They lived for a while in a tent in Sacramento Park, then later in a succession of small apartments. Yumi gave birth to a daughter that summer.

Masajiro decided not to rebuild his restaurant. He was tired of city life, of the mobsters who pressured honest businessmen to pay for

group by name, its intent was obvious. Ever since the Gold Rush of 1849, white workers in the Western states had seen Asians arrive in increasing numbers to find a place in the American economy. During hard times, competition for jobs brought racial tensions to the surface. A wave of anti-Chinese feelings sparked violence in the 1870s and '80s and prompted Congress to pass the Chinese Exclusion Act of 1882 (see p. 53).

Over the following decades, Japanese immigrants faced similar resentment. In 1906, the San Francisco school board segregated all Japanese, Chinese and Korean children into an "Oriental" school. When the Japanese government protested, Pres. Theodore Roosevelt offered a deal: He would reverse the school policy if Japan agreed to let only professionals of certain categories emigrate to the United States. The so-called Gentlemen's Agreement prevented an international confrontation, but bias against the Japanese in California increased. The 1913 alien land law was designed to make people like Yumi and Masajiro Kataoka permanent outsiders.

Above. Sox *(second row from bottom, third from left)* was small for her age in the second grade.

Opposite page. Japanese Americans left most of their possessions behind as they boarded trains to the internment camps.

"protection." He and Yumi and their new baby left San Francisco, and Masajiro made a fresh start as a tenant farmer. He saw a bright future in strawberry farming and hoped one day to own some land.

Back in the early 1900s, chemical fertilizers weren't as common as they are today. Strawberry crops could be grown in the same ground for only about three years before the essential soil nutrients were used up. If Masajiro had owned a big farm, he could have shifted his crops around. Since he was a tenant, he had to move to where the berries would grow. So he and his family lived lightly on the land. They didn't stay in one place long enough to put down roots.

In 1913, the state of California dashed Masajiro's hope of ever owning his own farm. A new law denied the right of land ownership to anyone who was not eligible to become a U.S. citizen. And, according to the federal Naturalization Law of 1790, only white immigrants were permitted to become naturalized citizens.

Although the California alien land law didn't mention the Japanese or any other

Farm life was hard work for the Kataokas. Yumi and Masajiro eventually had six children, and all of them had chores to do before and after school. Tsuyako, the youngest daughter, was born in 1918. She got her nickname, "Sox," from white friends who couldn't pronounce her real name. The nickname made her feel more American. Sox remembers that there was no Saturday or Sunday or Monday in the strawberry business, only Workday. And she remembers that no matter how difficult and tiring the labor, her mother was usually singing.

The Kataoka children spoke Japanese with their parents and English at school. A Japanese community school held afternoon classes in Japanese, but three miles was too far to walk home after dark. Most of what Sox and her siblings learned about their heritage they learned at home. The Kataokas were Buddhists, and frequently the Buddhist priest from Alameda came to conduct services in their living room for anyone who wanted to attend.

Masajiro's favorite Japanese tradition was the celebration of the New Year. It lasted a whole week, with lots of company, and Yumi spent long hours in the kitchen preparing Japanese foods to serve the guests. The house had to be spotlessly clean before midnight on New Year's Eve, with new wallpaper to symbolize a new beginning.

These practices reminded the Kataokas of their roots, but they mainly considered themselves Americans. Masajiro and Yumi were proud that all their offspring were American citizens. Masajiro didn't want to go back to Japan to live, but he did promise himself that one day he would return for a visit — one day when he wasn't so busy.

In 1932 Masajiro began renting farmland from a Mrs. Perkins, a strong-willed pioneer rancher whose family owned one of the largest rose nurseries in the world. Mrs. Perkins didn't make Masajiro sign a contract for the land. She even let him build his own house on it. She hired Sox's older sister, Nobuko, to work in her big ranch house. Nobuko got her nickname, "Nee," from the Perkins children, who were tall for their ages and considered her tiny. Nee cooked and cleaned and performed many more tasks than were expected of her, such as chopping firewood. In fact, she was such a vigorous worker that after she married and moved away, everyone else Mrs. Perkins hired seemed lazy by comparison.

Masajiro Kataoka died in late 1940. In keeping with Buddhist tradition, Yumi had his body cremated. Since he had always wanted to see Japan again, Yumi and Nee decided to take his ashes back for burial in Yamaguchi. They went in the late fall of 1941. At that time,

World War II was raging in Europe, and many feared that conflict would soon erupt between the U.S. and Japan. Nee and her mother got back to California just before that fear came true.

On Sunday morning, December 7, 1941, Sox, her sister Lillian and their mother were riding in the car. A special bulletin on the radio announced that the Japanese had mounted a surprise air attack on the U.S. Naval base at Pearl Harbor, Hawaii. The girls translated the news for Yumi. "This is terrible," Yumi said to them in Japanese. Because she was an Issei ("first generation" Japanese immigrant),

she was not a U.S. citizen. Her native country was now the enemy.

Sox and Lillian knew that their lives were about to change. They were Americans, born on American soil. They listened to the same music, followed the same fashions, pledged allegiance to the same flag as everyone else. But now they wondered how other Americans would treat them. They wondered if the storekeepers would still sell them food. Over the next few weeks, shops in towns around the area began posting signs telling Japanese customers to stay away. Old hostilities found new expression in the name of patriotism. There were scattered incidents of violence against Japanese Americans and their property.

The Kataokas had a mailbox at the post office in Centerville. Every morning, Sox went in to pick up the mail. After the Pearl Harbor attack, the postmaster began holding the family's mail at the window instead of putting it in the box, so that Sox had to come and ask him for it. This way, he could ask her questions, such as "How do you feel about the bombing?" or "What do you think is going to happen to you people?" Sox hated this daily confrontation. She kept her answers short and left as quickly as possible.

The question about what was going to happen was partially answered on February 19, 1942. Pres. Franklin D. Roosevelt on that day issued Executive Order 9066, establishing "military areas" along the West Coast and limiting the activities of "any or all persons" within them. Two months later, Civilian Exclusion Order No. 27 narrowed the focus of the restrictions by announcing that "all persons of Japanese ancestry, both alien and non-alien," would be "excluded" from the West Coast. Even Nisei ("second generation"), or those born in America to Japanese parents, were now unwelcome. The order disrupted the lives of 112,000 people, two-thirds of them U.S. citizens.

Evacuation orders posted on telephone poles and public buildings declared that Japanese Americans had one week to prepare to leave their homes. In the meantime, they had to abide by an 8 p.m. curfew and get permits to travel.

The instructions didn't tell people where they would be going, but they did tell them what to bring: only the bare necessities, like clothing and linens and soap. When someone said they could take what they could carry in two hands, the Kataokas took this literally. They had never owned suitcases, so they got a permit to go to a nearby town and buy two each — flimsy cardboard ones, outrageously priced.

Deciding what to pack was easy; getting rid of the rest was not. Anything obviously Japanese could be interpreted as a sign of collaboration with the enemy. Yumi Kataoka burned her family's Japanese books and letters, advertising calendars from Japanese businesses, even her certificates from a Japanese bank. Many people burned family keepsakes such as photographs and antique kimonos.

As for their other possessions, the evacuees had two choices: either leave them to be stolen or sell them at the going rate. One of Yumi's sons sold two cars, a long-bed truck and a Caterpillar tractor for a fraction of their worth. The Kataokas got $15 for their piano, and Sox was so happy to see it going home with someone that she gave the buyer all her sheet music and even threw her tennis racket into the bargain. Some people in the valley refused to trade their brand new stoves or refrigerators for pocket change, so they stored them in the Japanese school building, in hopes of retrieving them when the war was over.

May 9, 1942, was leaving day. A few days beforehand, Mrs. Perkins got in touch with Nee and told her to bring her whole family to the ranch house for a farewell breakfast. The invitation meant a lot to the Kataokas because most of the other white people they knew had shunned them. That morning, Mrs. Perkins ushered them into her beautiful formal dining room. The long table was set with her best china and crystal

Right. Evacuees could bring only what would fit into a suitcase.

Opposite page. No one knew where the crowded trucks would take them.

and silver. She usually had someone to cook and serve meals for her, but this time she did everything herself. When Nee and Sox offered to help her bring the food out, she told them that now it was her turn to serve.

After breakfast, Mrs. Perkins drove the Kataokas in her Oldsmobile to the grounds of the Japanese school, where buses were waiting. The fellow who ran the local hamburger stand was the only other white person who came to say goodbye. It hurt Sox's feelings that her close friends didn't show up, but she decided the reason was that they were afraid.

Yumi Kataoka had moved her family many times, but never like this. The bus let them out at Tanforan Racetrack in San Bruno, Calif. No one knew what to expect. None of the Kataokas had even been to a racetrack before. Inside, military policemen searched each person. All suitcases were opened and ransacked. A nurse peered into every eye and down every throat.

On the infield of the track stood new, army-style barracks. Sox said that she wanted to stay in those, but the officer said they

were for mothers with infants. He led the Kataokas around back to the stables: Their new home was a horse stall.

The building contained two back-to-back rows of 10 stalls each. Five adults — Sox and her three brothers and their mother — had a 9- by 20-foot enclosure to share. Manure littered the dirt floor. The walls had been recently whitewashed, but carelessly, so that horsehair and dirt were smeared in. And the walls reached only halfway to the roof — there were no ceilings. The nearest bathroom was a long walk away.

Sox worried about how her mother would take such humiliation. She was proud of Yumi for keeping the hurt hidden, for acting as if this were just another move. She knew that keeping the family together was Yumi's biggest concern.

The officers passed out cloth sacks for everyone to fill with hay for mattresses. Lunch that first day — served in a room lined with rough plank tables and benches — consisted of discolored cold cuts, overboiled Swiss chard and moldy bread. Sox refused to eat a bite.

In the dark stall that night, listening to the noises of all the other people, Sox couldn't fall asleep. She couldn't stop wondering what any of them had done to deserve being penned up like animals. She couldn't believe this was happening in America.

It didn't take Sox long to learn the local routine, including how early she had to get up to find an empty tub in the laundry shed. Her brothers washed dishes in the mess hall. There were long lines everywhere — for the toilets, for the laundry, for food. As clothing wore out, people shopped by mail from the Sears Roebuck catalog.

Occasionally, Mrs. Perkins came to visit. When she saw the damp dirt floor of the drafty stall, she went home and ripped up the linoleum from the Kataokas' kitchen

DOCUMENT

Confidential

After some Japanese Americans attempted to challenge the internment policy in the courts, the War Relocation Authority included the following statements in a confidential internal memo on August 12, 1942.

The action taken with respect to Japanese in this country is justifiable on the grounds of military necessity for several reasons.

1. All Japanese look very much alike to a white person — it is hard for us to distinguish between them. It would be hard to tell a Japanese soldier in disguise from a resident Japanese. The danger of infiltration by Japanese parachutists, soldiers, etc. is, therefore, reduced and the chances of detecting any attempt at infiltration are increased.

2. ... Many Japanese-Americans have been educated in Japan. Many, believers in Shintoism, worship the Emperor and regard his orders as superior to any loyalty they may owe the United States. Therefore, the action has reduced the danger of successful invasion by removing an element of the population which had never been assimilated and which might give way to their true feelings in the event that Japanese troops should land on our shores.

and brought it to them. She didn't want Yumi's rheumatism to get worse. Another time, she took Sox's broken wristwatch to have it repaired.

For four long months, daydreams and small acts of kindness made their internment bearable. Every night, Sox wondered what the next day would bring. There was very little official news about the government's plans, so rumors were the main source of information.

Late in the summer a rumor went around that the Japanese were going to be moved inland, to a concentration camp in the desert. Everyone started ordering high-top boots from the catalog — there were scorpions and snakes out there. According to some people, once they got to the new location, the government was going to drop a bomb on them.

Some of the rumors turned out to be true. At the end of the summer, Sox, Yumi and the other Japanese were packed into buses and driven east into the desert. Sox had never seen a place as dry and dusty and lifeless as Topaz, Utah. It looked like the surface of the moon. But when she saw the rows and rows of new barracks, some of them still unfinished, she could have kissed the ground. She reasoned

She couldn't stop wondering what any of them had done to deserve being penned up like animals.

that if the government was spending the time and money to build housing for her people, then it must not be planning to kill them.

The Kataokas' new quarters measured 20 by 24 feet — a little roomier than the horse stall and a lot cleaner. A single naked light bulb hung from the ceiling. In the corner stood a pot-bellied stove. By stringing up a few sheets, family members could carve out the illusion of privacy. The communal bathroom had six toilets and no doors.

There were no chairs or tables. People

Right, above and below. Horse stalls housed Japanese Americans at Tanforan Assembly Center.

Opposite page. Internees wait to be processed as armed guards keep watch from the towers.

scoured the construction site for materials. In just a short time, many families skillfully fashioned whole sets of furniture from orange crates and scrap lumber. Later, some residents laid out beautiful rock gardens on the barren ground.

Even in this strange new environment, much about camp life was familiar — the crowded living space, the boredom, the long lines for every necessity. But Sox began to notice changes in the people around her. In the dining hall, children made friends quickly and sat together in groups. The family meal — a central part of Japanese life — was losing its importance. A deeper toll resulted from unemployment: Fathers, no longer breadwinners, began to lose their self-respect and, sometimes, the respect of their families. Everyone was aimless now. Everyone was a small step from stir-crazy.

Camp residents had to pull together to avert despair. They formed social clubs and choirs and sports teams. They started newsletters to share information and ideas.

Sox had the good fortune to get a job as assistant block manager. She was responsible for looking after about 200 people in 72 rooms. The managers met every morning to discuss the needs of their residents. Extremes of

climate caused many problems, since temperatures often reached well below zero in the winter and over 100 in the summer months. Food was another source of complaint. The animal innards such as liver, gizzard, tongue, brains and chitterlings that made up much of the meat ration were foreign to the Japanese diet. Sox found them sickening. When the quality of meat improved after a while, Sox decided that the project director must have figured out that her people were human.

The block manager meetings gave Sox and the others some sense of value. But everywhere they looked, barbed wire and police patrols and curfews and watchtowers with armed guards constantly reminded them of their status.

The word around camp was "Don't go near the fence." Most of the military policemen were fresh out of combat duty, and they did not hesitate to use their weapons. At Topaz one day, a man was picking some wildflowers along the barbed wire. A guard yelled "Halt!" but the man was hard of hearing. He kept on picking and was shot. And once, a grandfather playing catch with his grandson went to retrieve the ball from just beyond the fence. The guard who killed him told authorities that

"A Grave Injustice"

On August 10, 1988, Congress enacted a law granting restitution payments for civilians interned during World War II.

SECTION. 2. Statement of the Congress

(a) With Regard to Individuals of Japanese Ancestry. — The Congress recognizes that, as described by the Commission on Wartime Relocation and Internment of Civilians, a grave injustice was done to both citizens and permanent resident aliens of Japanese ancestry by the evacuation, relocation, and internment of civilians during World War II. As the Commission documents, these actions were carried out without adequate security reasons and without any acts of espionage or sabotage documented by the Commission, and were motivated largely by racial prejudice, wartime hysteria, and a failure of political leadership. The excluded individuals of Japanese ancestry suffered enormous damages, both material and intangible, and there were incalculable losses in education and job training, all of which resulted in significant human suffering for which appropriate compensation has not been made. For these fundamental violations of the basic civil liberties and constitutional rights of these individuals of Japanese ancestry, the Congress apologizes on behalf of the Nation.

the old man had tried to escape.

As the war in Europe and the Pacific intensified, the government realized that many potentially able soldiers were sitting idle in the camps. In early 1943 Pres. Roosevelt wrote to the Secretary of War and contradicted his earlier Executive Order: "Americanism is not, and never was, a matter of race or ancestry. Every loyal American citizen should be given the opportunity to serve this country ... in the ranks of our armed forces."

By means of a "loyalty questionnaire," Uncle Sam began recruiting Nisei. In all, more than 30,000 Japanese Americans joined the service during the war. Others protested that they wouldn't serve until their families were allowed to return to the West Coast. About 300 so-called "no-no boys" refused to pledge their loyalty and were jailed for draft resistance. The questionnaire was also used as a means of releasing internees into the work force. In the camps, this process — however objectionable — stirred the first hopes of freedom.

On November 11, 1944, Pres. Roosevelt lifted the Civilian Exclusion Order. A month later, the government announced that the internment camps would be closed within a year.

Sox married a young man named Tom Kitashima in August 1945, just as the bombing of Hiroshima and Nagasaki brought the war to its conclusion. The camp supervisor offered her a job helping to process the closure of the camp. But since there wasn't a job for Tom, Sox said she couldn't stay. Even so, the supervisor found her a good position in San Francisco.

A few nights before Sox and Tom were set to leave Topaz, the supervisor and his wife invited them out for dinner and a cowboy movie in the town of Delta, 16 miles from the camp. There were rules against this kind of socializing, but the white couple didn't seem to care. The supervisor also gave them a blanket for the cold train ride to San Francisco — the government was using old dilapidated railroad cars to relocate the internees. On an October morning in 1945, Sox repacked the suitcase she had been living out of for three years and four months.

Yumi Kataoka, now 60 years old, prepared to move one more time. People were heading in all directions — there was nothing left to go back to. Yumi joined a large group headed for a housing center at Richmond, Calif. In time, Yumi and her scattered children heard reports from the valley that used to be their home. The Japanese school building had been emptied of all the stored appliances. The house that Masajiro had built on Mrs. Perkins' place was gone now, along with all the little things the family left behind. Someone told them that the old strawberry fields had been planted over with roses.

Shortly after the war was over, the government began considering ways to compensate Japanese Americans for their internment. In 1947, all Japanese American draft resisters received a presidential pardon. The following year, the Evacuation Claims Act provided partial repayment for lost or destroyed property, but the slow processing of claims drew widespread criticism.

Gradually, pressure mounted for new laws to guarantee that nothing like the relocation program could ever happen again. During the Bicentennial celebration in 1976, Pres. Gerald Ford revoked Executive Order 9066 and formally apologized to Japanese Americans. Four years later, the Commission on Wartime Relocation and Internment of Civilians began its investigation, which resulted in passage of the Civil Liberties Act of 1988.

Under the provisions of this law, each surviving internee received $20,000 as a symbolic reparation for their hardship. The law also provided compensation for the Aleut people of Alaska who were relocated from their island homes after a Japanese invasion. In addition, the act established a fund for educating the public about the internment experience. ◆

On the Home Front

Enemy is a powerful word. Most of us could name a few people we don't like. In a debate or on the basketball court, we square off against our opponents. When we apply for a job or run for office, we hope to outperform our rivals. Life is full of small battles, but few of us have what we would call real enemies.

War is a different story. When Congress declares war — or the President sends troops into a foreign conflict — another country, officially or unofficially, becomes "the enemy." In some cases, such as World War II, the sense of physical danger or moral outrage is so widespread that practically every American — both on and off the battlefield — feels a personal stake in the struggle. Other conflicts, such as the one in Vietnam, have divided our nation and failed to create a common perception of "the enemy."

Every military engagement is a struggle on the home front as well as on the front line. In addition to the concerns of the war itself, Americans must decide how to treat their fellow citizens who have ties to the foreign foe. Conflict with other countries can bring out hidden prejudices in our own neighborhoods.

Often in our history, war has caused certain Americans to be treated as "them":

• Prejudice against British immigrants lasted for decades after the War of 1812.

• During World War I, German, Austrian, Hungarian and Russian

Americans experienced harassment and intimidation. The German Hutterites (see p. 13) were persecuted for their anti-war views.

• After the Japanese attack on Pearl Harbor, Japanese Americans found themselves first shunned and harassed, then rounded up and stripped of their rights. German and Italian Americans experienced job discrimination and social prejudice but no infringements by the government. Most historians explain the contrasting treatment of Japanese and European Americans in terms of underlying racism brought to the surface by the war.

• As the Cold War developed between the U.S. and the communist Soviet Union after World War II, many Americans were falsely accused of involvement in "communist plots" within the government. Sen. Joseph McCarthy in 1950 launched a notorious campaign to expose this alleged subversion (see p. 10). Many innocent people lost their jobs and their reputations on the basis of false charges.

• In the early 1950s, China's support of North Korea in the Korean War brought discrimination against Chinese Americans. They were prohibited from sending money to relatives in China. In urban Chinatowns, immigration officers conducted raids in search of illegal aliens.

• The Vietnam War of the 1960s and '70s stirred sometimes violent hostility between those Americans who supported U.S. involvement and those who opposed it. War-related racism also had a lingering effect. In some areas, immigrants from Southeast Asia faced harassment as "gooks." In 1989, a white man in Raleigh, N. C., killed Chinese American Jim Loo outside a pool hall after mistaking him for a Vietnamese. The murderer said that several of his friends had died in Vietnam.

• Three separate developments — the Arab oil embargo of the early 1970s, a wave of Arab- and Muslim-related terrorism, and the Persian Gulf War of 1991 — contributed to a rise in prejudice and hate crimes against Arab Americans.

Nightriding with the Klan

TIGER KNOWLES SPENT MUCH OF his childhood in the 1960s criss-crossing the South, stopping wherever his father could find construction work. He frequently found himself alone in new surroundings. It was hard to make friends and keep them. His only siblings, seven half-brothers from his dad's first marriage, lived with their mother.

Tiger grew up feeling like an outsider, with all the fears and insecurities that come with that. When he was 7, he was beaten up by

Since 1865, the white robes and burning crosses of the Ku Klux Klan have been symbols of organized hatred in America. Klan members in nearly every state have committed acts of violence against others simply because of their race, nationality, religion or lifestyle. Although the traditional Klan declined in the years following the civil rights movement, its ideas did not die. By 1993, there were more than 300 different white supremacist organizations actively recruiting in the U.S.

For the members of these groups, the organized hate movement offers an outlet for anger, a rationalization for racism and the illusion of superiority. For Tiger Knowles in the early 1980s, a tattered remnant of the Klan became a family.

several black teenagers. His mom started walking with him to school. Three years later, another group of blacks tried to cut him with a broken bottle. Tiger got away, but for the next several days he pretended he was sick and stayed home.

By the time Tiger moved with his family to the south Alabama town of Mobile, he was accustomed to rejection. He hated school so much that he dropped out in the 8th grade.

At 14, Tiger desperately needed a place where he could fit in. One day while he was driving his father's car he was approached at an intersection by some people raising money for an organization called the UKA, the United Klans of America. The people were nice to him and invited him to one of their meetings over in Theodore.

Tiger went. At the meeting, he met Henry Hays, the

Tiger Knowles

Kligripp, or secretary, of Unit 900. Henry was 10 years older than Tiger and had grown up in the Klan. His father, Bennie Jack Hays, was the unit's Grand Titan and had been a Klansman for 50 years. Henry's brother-in-law Frank Cox was the Exalted Cyclops, second in command. Tiger decided to join.

Henry Hays was the informal leader of the younger Klansmen, including Tiger, Teddy Kyzar and Matt Jones. Matt held the title of Kludd. He read "the big old oath" that opened every meeting and measured new Klansmen for their robes and hoods. After the Klavern meetings next to Bennie's house in Theodore, the three young men would often get together at Henry's apartment in Mobile. For a year, Tiger lived there.

Tiger rose quickly through the ranks of the local UKA. He served as Klokard, or chaplain, for a while and, by 1981, at the age of 17, had attained the rank of Province Klaliff. As PK, he was second in command over the Klan units of south Alabama. He supervised activities that were considered military in nature, such as burning crosses.

Tiger also participated in the initiation of new members. Klan initiation was a solemn ceremony conducted according to complicated rules. Every new member had to swear to uphold the "God-given supremacy of the white race." The Klansman's Manual stated that "This country was founded by the finest elements of the White Race. This government was established by the same superior types of the white race. They passed it on to posterity to be maintained by white men as a white man's country for the white race."

The initiation ceremony included an oath of secrecy that prohibited any Klansman from discussing Klan business with aliens (anyone not affiliated with the Klan). The penalties for breaking that oath varied. Once, when Teddy Kyzar admitted he told an alien about something that had happened during a Klan meeting, he was forced to bend over the ceremonial altar and was then beaten with a paddle.

The Klansmen had strict rules for themselves and even more rigid expectations of others. They considered it their job to send a message, usually in the form of a burning cross, to aliens who deviated from Klan values. Tiger was among the Klansmen who burned a cross in the front yard of a man who was known to be cheating on his wife.

Klan threats came in other forms as well. Tiger and several others once slashed the tires of cars belonging to homosexuals. On Herndon Avenue, the street where Henry lived, they slashed tires at a predominantly black apartment complex.

Tiger's self-confidence surged when he had another person's life in his hands. He and Henry Hays drove into downtown Mobile late one night to an area where gay men gathered. They picked up a man and, after he got in the car, pulled a knife on him and held him down in the rear floorboard, while they debated whether to cut his throat or throw him off a boat in Mobile Bay.

Tiger drove over the Causeway out to a wooded area off County Road 225 where people had dumped old refrigerators and other trash. They made their captive get out and take his clothes off and then get down on the ground. When he got back up, Henry took the knife and sawed off a twist of the man's beard. Henry and Tiger told him to imagine what the rusty old knife was going to feel like on his throat. They told him they had a rifle with a night scope, so he might as well not try anything.

The night air was damp and cold. Henry

> *Tiger's self-confidence surged when he had another person's life in his hands.*

Right. A Klan diagram shows the ritual layout of a Klavern hall.

Opposite page. The Klavern of Unit 900 was a rundown building in Bennie Hays' backyard.

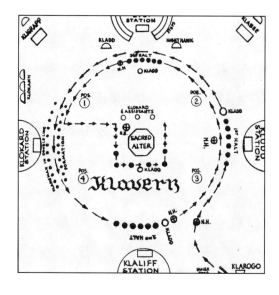

hit the man hard under the rib cage and Tiger told him he'd better make his peace with his maker. When Tiger and Henry turned away for a second, the man took off running naked through the dark woods. They didn't have that rifle. They just let him run.

During the third week of March 1981, Frank Cox decided it was time to show the newcomer, Teddy Kyzar, how to stage a cross burning. At a meeting that week, the Klansmen discovered the perfect opportunity.

In Unit 900, it was one member's responsibility to keep a scrapbook of news clippings and other items of interest to the Klan. At the third weekly meeting that March, Red Betancourt read from his scrapbook an article about a black man named Josephus Anderson who was being tried in Mobile for killing a white police officer in Birmingham. The jury in this trial consisted of 11 blacks and one white, and no one at Unit 900 expected a conviction. Even the idea of blacks on juries disgusted the members of Unit 900.

After Red finished reading the clipping, Bennie Hays told Henry, the Kligripp, to "get this down." He said if a black can get away with killing a white cop, then a white should be able to get away with killing a black. Red said blacks were so dumb they all needed to be killed.

After the meeting, Bennie, Henry and Tiger continued the discussion at Bennie's house. Tiger said, "I wonder what people would think if they found a nigger hanging in Mobile." Henry and Tiger thought Herndon Avenue, near Henry's apartment in a racially mixed part of town, would be the right place to leave this kind of message. Bennie Hays, who happened to be selling an apartment building he owned on that street, warned them not to do anything until the sale went through. He didn't want a hanging to scare the buyer away.

On Friday afternoon, March 20, Tiger got the go-ahead. Henry told him that the sale had been completed. Around supper time, Henry and Tiger drove to Frank Cox's trailer on

"What Has Happened to America?"

Klan groups frequently leave pamphlets on doorsteps and parked cars to spread their message of hate. A group calling itself the Bristol Knights distributed a flier in white Connecticut neighborhoods in the 1980s.

Dear Homeowner,

I saw the for sale sign in front of your home. Hopefully, the American dream is coming true for you and your family. You are selling your home and moving into a bigger, more beautiful one. ...

The truth, so many times, is that Americans are being forced from their homes. They must sell out their dream. ...

What has happened to America in 30 short years? Is it our destiny to decline as other great nations have in the past? ... Only you can save America. I don't care if you know some good non-whites. The White Race built this nation, and ever since we let the flood gates open to non-white immigrants and gave non-whites "equal rights" we have been declining.

If you think it's bad now, wait till the minority becomes the majority. And at the rate they're multiplying, and immigrating here, it won't be long. We don't have to allow that to happen. America is our country!

Gunn Road and asked him if he knew where they could find some rope. Frank got in Henry's car and took them first to his grandmother's house nearby, but she wasn't home. Then he took them to his parents' house a little further on. Frank told his mother that Tiger's mother's station wagon had died on the interstate and they had to tow it. Frank's mother told him to help himself to some rope in the boat shed.

Frank brought out 20 feet of half-inch nylon anchor rope and got back in the car. He handed the rope over the seat to Tiger, who flicked his lighter and burned the ends of the rope to keep them from unraveling. Then he formed a loop at one end and began making small laps to close the loop.

Henry dropped Frank off at his home and drove deeper into the trailer park to where Matt Jones lived. Matt was underage, but Frank Cox had recently bought him a blue steel snubnose .22-caliber pistol. Henry and Tiger asked Matt if they could borrow the gun, and he let them. On the way back to Herndon Avenue, Tiger carefully counted the number of coils as he wrapped, stopping at 13. Tying hangman's nooses was an old hobby of his. Henry and Tiger got to Henry's apartment around 9:45.

As usual, there were a lot of people at Henry's. Teddy Kyzar was there, and various neighbors. Linda from across the street had brought her baby girl over and put her to bed in Henry and Denise's room. Up front was a running Spades game. Cigarette smoke and the racket from the TV and stereo periodically sent people to the porch to clear their heads.

The 10 o'clock news came on with the announcement of a hung jury in the Josephus Anderson trial. Although the district attorney could decide to hold a retrial, to the Klansmen it appeared that a black man accused of killing a white policeman was going to go free. No one in Henry's apartment was pleased with this news, but the Klansmen held their rage until they were out of the aliens' presence.

Shortly after they heard the news, Tiger and Henry left in Henry's black and red 1962 Buick Wildcat. They had a mis-

sion to perform. They were determined to show Mobile that what happened in that courtroom was wrong.

They drove around in a black part of town for about an hour, looking for a man — any black man — by himself with no one else in view. They spotted an old man at a pay phone, but he was too far from the curb, and the telephone was a problem. They drove some more and agreed that if they couldn't find anyone in the next few blocks, they'd call off their search for the night.

Then they saw a young black man walking alone. Henry pulled up next to him, and Tiger asked if he could tell them how to get to Powell's, a local nightclub. When the man approached the car, Tiger showed him the snubnose .22-caliber pistol and told him to stay quiet. Tiger got out of the car and ordered the man into the back seat, then got in beside him. He looked to be about Tiger's age. It would be the next day before Tiger and Henry learned the man's name: Michael Donald.

Henry drove toward Baldwin County along the old truck route by the paper mills. On the causeway that crossed the Bay, Tiger told Michael to empty his pockets onto the rear floorboard. Michael kept saying, "I don't believe this is happening. You can do anything you want to me. Just let me go."

Henry asked Michael if he had heard about the recent murders of black children in Atlanta. Michael said he had, and Henry responded, "Well, you could wind up just like them." He turned in at the same garbage dump where they had taken the gay man.

"Please don't kill me," Michael said. "I'll do anything you want. Just don't kill me."

Everyone got out of the car. Michael lunged at Tiger, and they both fell down. Henry piled on. Michael grabbed the St. Christopher medal Tiger wore around his neck and broke the chain.

"I'll kill you for that," Tiger said. They scuffled in the sandy dirt. Tiger lost his grip on the gun and it was knocked away. Michael grabbed a tree limb, three or four

Klan recruiting
posters and literature
keep alive the
dramatic image of
the nightrider.

feet long, and started swinging it, but he couldn't hold onto it. Tiger grabbed the limb and began beating Michael, over and over, until Michael lay on the ground gasping for breath.

Tiger held Michael down while Henry got the noose from the car. It took Tiger and Henry both to get the loop over Michael's head. Henry stood and braced his foot against Michael's forehead to cinch the loop tight. Then he ran the rope out to its full length and tugged. Henry was trying to drag him, but Michael kept rising up on his knees, so Tiger struck him again with the limb. The pulling tired Henry, so he and Tiger switched places

for a while. It was only when Michael finally quit struggling that they were able to drag him to the car.

They put him on his back in the trunk, then Henry took his utility knife and made three slits in Michael's throat just above the noose.

"Why are you doing that?" Tiger said. "He's dead."

"I just wanted to make sure," Henry said.

Henry closed the trunk, and they scraped some tree branches over the ground to cover their tracks. Tiger remembered the lost gun. They searched until they found it. Then Tiger and Henry brushed off each other's clothes

---

IN CONTEXT

The Circle of Hate

The Ku Klux Klan that Tiger Knowles and Henry Hays belonged to was a faded remnant of an organization that once boasted more than 4 million members nationwide. But the first Klan meeting — in December 1865 — was as small as the backyard meetings of Unit 900.

Still stinging from General Lee's surrender nine months earlier, six young Confederate veterans gathered in a Pulaski, Tenn., law office to form a secret social club. They took the name Ku Klux from the Greek word meaning "circle." At first, the group won a reputation for elaborate pranks designed to frighten blacks newly freed from slavery.

Mischief turned to violence, however, as the growing Klan sought to preserve white supremacy in the face of Northern insistence that the Civil War had ended the social inequalities of the Old South. Using terrorist tactics such as night raids, beatings and lynchings of blacks and their white supporters, Klan members across the South effectively challenged the program of Reconstruction.

An order issued by the Klan's reputed leader, former Confederate Gen. Nathan Bedford Forrest, for the national group to disband in 1869 —

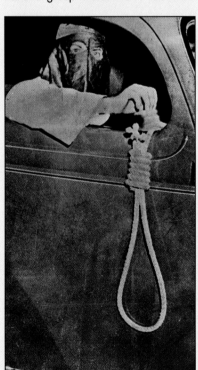

at the height of its influence — has been variously interpreted by historians. Some think that Forrest disapproved of the increasing violence, while others allege that he was only trying to

avoid personal accountability for it. Congress enacted several anti-Klan laws, but the real decline of the original Klan reflects the fact that by the mid-1870s the group's main goal — the restoration of white government — had been achieved.

It was partly the Leo Frank trial (see p. 66) that inspired a group of Georgians to revive the name Ku Klux Klan in 1915. A steady stream of immigration from Europe gave Protestant whites new groups to resent and to fear and to hate. As an outgrowth of the nativist movement, the second Klan waged its war of terror against "foreigners," Catholics, Jews and organized labor, in addition to its traditional enemy, blacks.

To the old Klan hallmarks of night rides, hooded robes and elaborate rituals, the new group added an astonishing symbol — the burning cross. Intended both to inspire whites and to frighten blacks, cross-burning was for Klansmen a means of proclaiming the "God-given supremacy of the white race." A massive recruitment campaign cast the Klan as the true defender of America's racial, religious and moral order.

and got in the car.

"He sure was tough," Henry said and smiled.

They drove first to Theodore to return the gun to Jones. There was still sand in the barrel. Then they decided to give Frank Cox a look at the body. At 12:30 a.m., the party on Herndon Avenue was still going.

Tiger threw Michael's wallet into a dumpster behind the apartments. When Henry and Tiger went in to get Frank, Teddy Kyzar followed them back out. Teddy told Tiger there was blood on his shirt, and Tiger pulled it off without unbuttoning it. Buttons popped off in the hallway. When Teddy asked where the

blood came from, Tiger told him they had "beat up a queer." Teddy asked if they'd take him along the next time they went after somebody. Frank offered Tiger a shirt from his car. Out back, Tiger took Teddy around the corner of the building while Henry lifted the trunk hood for Frank.

Several times that night, Henry went out and walked around the building. Inside, the Spades game was still running. There was still plenty to eat, and Linda had gone over to her place and brought back some Kool-Aid.

Around 1:30, Tiger told Frank to take Teddy and go light the cross. Frank had brought the cross with him from Unit 900 and

Opposite page. Secrecy and intimidation form the core of Klan activity.

Below. Many neo-Nazi Skinhead groups adopt ideas as well as emblems from the Klan.

Membership surged in the Midwest as well as the South, reaching a peak in the 1920s. During that decade, the Klan became a highly visible and widely accepted part of American life. In 1925, for example, 40,000 Klan members gathered for a march in Washington, D.C.

The Depression of the 1930s brought a sharp decline in Klan activity, and charges of tax evasion forced the group to disband in 1944. Twenty years later, however, the civil rights movement aroused a renewal of organized racism by numerous factions that included 'Klan' in their names. Bombings, beatings and lynchings during this period echoed the terrorism of a century before.

Despite Klan efforts, the civil rights struggle produced lasting changes in Southern society. As a consequence, the various Klans dwindled, and in-fighting fragmented the movement even further. Nevertheless, several events, including the murder of

Michael Donald in 1981, brought the Klan back into the national spotlight:

• In 1979, former neo-Nazi and Klan organizer David Duke made an unsuccessful but widely publicized bid for the Louisiana Senate. Ten years later, he attempted to refine his image and won a seat in the state legislature. His subsequent

campaigns for state and national office met with heated controversy and, ultimately, defeat.

• In 1981, Klansmen openly harassed Vietnamese fishermen in Galveston Bay in Texas until a court order ended the campaign of intimidation.

• During the early 1980s, the FBI, Klanwatch and other monitors of hate-group activity reported a growing paramilitary movement within Klan organizations.

• In 1987, a Klan-led mob attacked civil rights marchers in all-white Forsyth County, Ga.

• In 1992, Klan members used harassment and threats of violence to hinder the integration of public housing in Vidor, Texas.

Today, a few thousand people claim membership in Klan-like groups, some of them allied with neo-Nazis and others who share their commitment to white supremacy.

Tiger Knowles

Henry Hays

Bennie Hays

Teddy Kyzar

Right. Tiger and Henry hoped the lynching of Michael Donald would send a message to both whites and blacks in Mobile.

stashed it in Tiger's pickup. Tiger went out back and filled a gallon milk jug with diesel fuel and put it in the truck.

Frank and Teddy drove the truck downtown and circled the courthouse three times. This was the same courthouse where earlier that night the jury had failed to convict Josephus Anderson. Frank said he wanted to put the cross on the side that faced the police station, but there was too much traffic. He let Teddy off, and Teddy set the cross up a foot and a half from the courthouse building. He doused it with diesel fuel and struck a match. He met Frank at the corner by the bridge, where they watched the flaming cross for just an instant before leaving.

The party at Henry and Denise's broke up a little after 4:00 a.m. A few minutes later, Henry and Tiger moved the Wildcat around to a hedge that skirted the sidewalk. The sky was still dark, but dawn wasn't far off. They took the body out of the trunk and laid it up against the hedge. A car came by, and Henry and Tiger stood perfectly still until it was gone. Then they carried the body across the street to a camphor tree that stood in a vacant lot.

Tiger tried to throw the loose end of the rope over a limb but kept missing. Henry finally got it over while Tiger lifted the body. They pulled on the rope, but they couldn't get the body to hang right because it had stiffened in a folded-up position in the trunk. Also, the limb wouldn't swing back high enough to keep Michael's feet off the ground. Michael's forehead still had a waffle-mark from Henry's boot sole.

When Henry and Tiger went back to the apartment, they stepped out on the porch to check the view. They could just barely see the body hanging on the camphor tree. Teddy Kyzar came out and punched Tiger in the side. "Good job, Tiger," he said. This bothered Tiger. Teddy wasn't supposed

Frank Cox

to know anything.

Henry and Tiger got little sleep before the sun came up and their Herndon Avenue neighbors saw what had happened during the night. When the commotion began, Henry called the television station to make sure the message got out. Then he called his father, Benny, and told him to come see what was going on. Bennie Hays floored his truck all the way from Theodore. On Herndon Avenue, he wheeled past the police barricade and drove up on the sidewalk in front of the apartment building.

Twenty-five police officers kept onlookers off the vacant lot. Police photographers took pictures of the body, dangling on its bent knees. It would be about an hour before a woman would discover Michael Donald's wallet in the dumpster and turn it over to the police. They would learn that he was a 19-year-old part-time mail-room worker at the *Mobile Register*. That he was the youngest of seven children and still lived with his mother, Beulah Mae. That he was training to be a bricklayer and considering signing up with the army. That on Friday night, March 20, 1981, he left his sister's house to buy a pack of cigarettes and never came home.

Two years after the lynching of Michael Donald, Henry Hays was convicted of murder and sentenced to death. Tiger Knowles was sent to prison for life.

Believing that her son's killing had been plotted within the Klan, Beulah Mae Donald sued the members of Unit 900 and the United Klans of America in civil court in 1987. Each day of the trial, she forced herself into the courtroom to hear testimony about the hatred and brutality that took her son away.

On the last day of the trial, Tiger Knowles was granted permission to speak in court. He stood before the jury box.

"I hope that people learn from my mistake," he said. "I've lost my family. I've got people after me." Knowles turned to face Mrs. Donald. "I can't bring your son back, but I'm sorry for what happened." He was weeping now. Mrs. Donald rocked in her seat.

"God knows if I could trade places with him, I would," Tiger continued. "Whatever it takes — I have nothing. But I will have to do

Beulah Mae Donald

it. And if it takes me the rest of my life to pay it, any comfort it may bring, I hope it will." Tears streamed down Tiger's face. Members of the jury were crying, and the judge wiped his eyes.

Beulah Mae Donald sat calm and still. She spoke softly. "I forgive you," she said. "From the day I found out who you all was, I asked God to take care of y'all, and He has."

That evening the jury ordered the United Klans of America to pay Mrs. Donald $7 million in damages. UKA assets fell far short of that amount, but the decision forced the organization out of existence. ◆

AT ISSUE

A Place to Fit In

We all need people who accept us and listen to us, people we can count on. For many fortunate individuals, the family is the first group to meet this need. Later in life, more good luck, along with good judgment, helps ensure that the other groups we fit into will be healthy ones.

Belonging to a group offers many benefits. As the old saying goes, there's strength in numbers. We can accomplish things in a group that we lack the ability or courage to do by ourselves.

Belonging teaches us the value of teamwork, of sharing the labor — and the credit — in achieving a goal. Group identity can be a great source of self-esteem and pride. It can help transform frustration and anger into productive energy. Another advantage of membership in a group is the personal support and guidance we get from our fellow members. We have a better chance at a decent life if we can learn from other people's experiences as well as our own.

But group membership has its risks, too. People come together in groups because they share something in common — a hobby, a goal, a problem, an interest. We take comfort in our similarities, but we can also use our group identity to reject others who are different, who don't "qualify" for our group.

The same impulse can cause us to enforce conformity among group members themselves, and to judge harshly those members who deviate from our standards. Pledges, uniforms, codes of behavior are all attempts to secure allegiance and mandate conformity within the group.

If we are not careful, we can allow our group identity to obscure our best judgment. In attempting to conform, we can go along with decisions we don't agree with and act in ways we know are wrong. We can rationalize our behavior as group loyalty and avoid taking responsibility for our actions. We conform because we're afraid of losing the security of the group and becoming an outsider.

Our need to belong can be so urgent that we fall under the control of peer pressure, one of the most powerful forces in the universe. The Nazi youth used group loyalty as a form of intimidation, in the same way Klan groups, Skinheads and street gangs do today.

Tiger Knowles looked up to Benny and Henry Hays. They helped him find somebody to look down on.

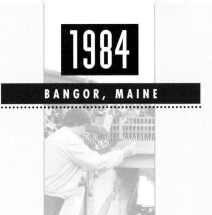

B Y THE TIME CHARLIE HOWARD
reached high school in the late 1970s,
he was accustomed to his classmates'
taunts and sneers. Charlie was fair-
haired and small-boned. He had a learning dis-
ability. His severe asthma would have made it
difficult for him to participate in sports, even if
he had wanted to. The way he walked and
talked set him apart from most of the other
boys in Portsmouth, N.H. As a little kid, he got
laughed at and called a "sissy." In later years,
he got shoved around and called a "fag."

A Rose for Charlie

*In the American colonies, anyone
convicted of committing a homosexual act
could be sentenced to death. Today, gays
and lesbians are the most frequent targets
of hate crimes. Data presented in 1986 to
the U.S. House Judiciary Subcommittee on
Criminal Justice showed that homosexuals
were four times more likely to be victims
of violence than persons in the general
population.*

*Like all bias crimes, anti-gay
offenses are aimed not just at their
individual victims but also at the
communities to which those individuals
belong. A brick through the window of a
lesbian couple's apartment sends a
message of hate to every gay person in
the area. Graffiti on the door of a church
that welcomes homosexuals is a warning
to everyone who believes in tolerance. A
physical assault on one gay man reminds
all others that their turn could be next.*

Charlie had to have a tough shell just to
get through most days without crying or running away. Underneath, he accumulated a lot
of scars and bruises. He wondered if people
would ever leave him alone — or if, because he
was gay, he would be the butt of their jokes
forever. Charlie couldn't wait to get out of
high school, but he skipped his graduation ceremony because he didn't want his
family to witness how the other students treated him.

Many new graduates see the
future as an open door. Charlie saw
doors closing. Since his grades
were low, he wasn't considered "college material."
Jobs were scarce in
Portsmouth, especially
for someone who
made no secret of
being homosexual.
He didn't get

Charlie Howard

"What Did I Do Wrong?"

A 27-year-old lesbian from Delaware recalls a typical encounter with homophobia.

One time before I came out, I was walking down the street with a woman I was tutoring. She was going to give me a ride home. These men approached us and surrounded us. They looked like fraternity guys. They started yelling and calling us "lezzies" and "dykes" and "freaks." It was scary. It was dark. There were just the two of us. We didn't respond to anything they had to say, and they had somewhere else to go. They just wanted to harass us. They just wanted to scare us. They thought it was funny.

We kept on walking. But how do you collect yourself after something like that happens? I was really angry. I felt helpless and wished I could have done something different. Those things kind of stick with you. That was before I came out. And deep down inside I wondered, 'How did they know? What did I do wrong?' It kind of fed my own homophobia. It lingered on and made the process of coming out that much harder. You think, 'If I come out, are they going to do that even more?'

along well with his stepfather, so he knew he couldn't continue to live at home. As long as he remained in Portsmouth, Charlie felt, he would be an embarrassment to his family.

Leaving town seemed to be his only option. He drifted around for a few years, into his early 20s, and the familiar hassles and put-downs followed wherever he went. He eventually moved in with a man in the small coastal town of Ellsworth, Maine. When this relationship broke up in early January 1984, Charlie decided that nearby Bangor, with a population of 30,000, offered better opportunities for work and for a social life.

A mutual friend introduced Charlie to Scott Hamilton and Paul Noddin, who lived in a big Victorian house they had restored on Highland Avenue in Bangor. Charlie had no money, no job and no

plans. Scott and Paul offered him a place to stay while he looked for work.

As the weeks passed, Charlie's prospects remained as bleak as the Bangor winter. The local job market wasn't what he had hoped for, and after a month Scott and Paul suggested that Charlie might be better off returning to Portsmouth, where he had more connections. Charlie's mother let him move back home.

The new arrangement didn't last a week. He moved in with another man, but that situation didn't work out either. He called Scott and Paul. They could hear the pain in Charlie's voice, so they decided to help him give Bangor another try.

Something was different this time. Charlie was more upbeat and determined, and his high spirits seemed to open more

attending services regularly and soon decided to undertake the preparation required for membership.

The Unitarian Church and Interweave were the only two organizations in Bangor that welcomed homosexuals. Many of the other churches, in fact, were openly hostile. Fundamentalist preachers used their pulpits to blame gays and lesbians for many of society's ills. There were no gay bars in town, and local clubs routinely kicked out couples of the same sex who tried to dance together. Most of Charlie's friends had experienced verbal harassment, and several had been physically attacked. Incidents of gay-bashing often went unreported because victims expected little support from the police.

As a newcomer in town, Charlie Howard ignored some of the unwritten rules observed by more long-term gay residents. He wore whatever he felt like, for instance, even if earrings and a shoulder bag and, occasionally, eye makeup weren't "acceptable" adornments for Bangor males. He liked to call people "dearie." In moments of joy or mischief or defiance, he could burst into song (usually "I Am What I Am," from the musical *La Cage Aux Folles*).

Refusing to camouflage himself in the crowd, Charlie drew the crowd's attention — and its anger. High school kids baited him with obscenities on the street. He got ejected from the West Market Disco for dancing with a man. One day in the grocery store a middle-aged woman suddenly started shouting at him, "You pervert! You queer!" Everyone stared. Charlie dropped his basket and walked slowly toward the door, terrified. Just before exiting, he choked back his fear, turned, and blew a kiss at the cluster of hateful faces.

This confrontation seemed to mark a turning point for Charlie. The stares of strangers began to spook him a little more after that. Sometimes he was afraid to leave his apartment. He stepped outside one morning and found his pet kitten lying dead on the doorstep. It had been strangled.

Refusing to camouflage himself in the crowd, Charlie drew the crowd's attention — and its anger.

doors. A neighbor helped him get a part-time job through a city employment program. He found a warm community of friends at the Unitarian Church, which had a number of openly gay members. The church also sponsored Interweave, a gay and lesbian support group.

As a token of thanks for their generosity, Charlie surprised Scott and Paul by decorating their house for Easter and cooking an elaborate meal. A few weeks later, he took a place of his own on the third floor of an old rooming-house on First Street, behind the church. The building was run-down, but Charlie livened his surroundings with posters and plants and, eventually, a kitten.

Church had never been a big part of Charlie's life, but the acceptance he felt among the Unitarians was a new experience. Here he found a place to express his own openness and sense of humor, his love for life. He started

Gay people in Bangor were accustomed to intolerance and exclusion.

"Not Proper Persons"

From the late 1940s to the mid-1950s, numerous government agencies participated in a campaign to remove homosexuals from federal employment. The Senate Subcommittee on Investigations issued a report on Dec. 15, 1950, outlining the reasons for this policy.

In the opinion of this subcommittee homosexuals ... are not proper persons to be employed in Government for two reasons; first, they are generally unsuitable, and second, they constitute security risks. ...

Aside from the criminality and immorality involved in sex perversion such behavior is so contrary to the normal accepted standards of social behavior that persons who engage in such activity are looked upon as outcasts by society generally. ...

As has been previously discussed in this report, the pervert is easy prey to the blackmailer. It follows that if blackmailers can extort money from a homosexual under the threat of disclosure, espionage agents can use the same type of pressure to extort confidential information or other material they might be seeking.

Since the initiation of this investigation considerable progress has been made in removing homosexuals and similar undesirable employees from ... positions in the Government.

Charlie's friends wished they could shield him from such cruelties, but they knew he would have to come to his own terms with a perilous world. He wasn't the only one for whom church and Interweave meetings sometimes felt like shelters in a storm.

Interweave sponsored a potluck supper on the night of Saturday, July 7, 1984. When the party broke up around 10 o'clock, Charlie talked his friend Roy Ogden into walking downtown with him to check his post office box. They headed up State Street. Midway across the bridge spanning Kenduskeag Stream, in the heart of Bangor, Charlie noticed a car slowing down just behind them. He thought it was one belonging to some high school boys who had harassed him a few days earlier. When they stopped the car and got out, he knew that he was right.

The three young men had just left a party to look for more beer when they spotted Charlie. Shawn Mabry, the driver, was a 16-year-old high school dropout who had recently been in trouble for using a nunchuk. Mabry was making a name for

himself in the city hockey league.

Daniel Ness, a year older than Shawn, lived with his family on the west side, the upper-class side of Bangor. His favorite subject was art.

Jim Baines, almost 16, managed to keep his grades up while playing football and basketball. He planned to go to college some day.

Two girls stayed behind in the car. One of them had a fake ID that she intended to use to buy the beer.

"Hey, fag!" one boy yelled. Then the three started running. Roy and Charlie took off, but Charlie tripped on the curb and fell hard onto the walkway. He couldn't get his breath: The excitement was making his asthma kick in. He felt his lungs jamming.

Charlie scrambled to stand, but the boys grabbed him. They threw him back down and laid into him with kicks and punches.

"Over the bridge!" shouted Jim Baines. Daniel grabbed Charlie under the arms and lifted. Jim got him by the legs.

Charlie was gasping now. He snatched enough air to yell, "I can't swim!" From the far end of the bridge, Roy heard his plea.

Jim and Daniel heaved Charlie up onto the guardrail. They had to pry his hands loose. Shawn gave the shove that sent him over. They looked down at the black water 20 feet below and congratulated themselves.

The girls in the car were grinding the ignition. They yelled for Jim and Daniel and Shawn to come on. The boys spotted Roy Ogden watching from the end of the bridge and promised him he'd be sorry if he ever told anyone. When they got back to the car, they were laughing.

Roy waited for the car to disappear. He could still hear the boys whooping and hollering. Then he ran along State Street till he found a fire alarm. In a few minutes, fire engines and police cars were screaming toward the bridge.

Through downtown Bangor, Kenduskeag Stream flows between smooth concrete walls. Its depth below the bridge that night was estimated at around 10 feet. The searchlights trained into the current and along the banks revealed no sign of Charlie Howard.

Around the country, the issue of gay rights has divided many communities.

The Colorado Plan

In 1992 Colorado became the first state in U.S. history to adopt a constitutional amendment denying civil rights to certain citizens. In 1994 the Colorado Supreme Court declared the amendment unconstitutional. Similar measures remained under consideration in several states.

Amendment 2

Neither the State of Colorado, through any of its branches or departments, nor any of its agencies, political subdivisions, municipalities or school districts, shall enact, adopt or enforce any statute, regulation, ordinance or policy whereby homosexual, lesbian or bi-sexual orientation, conduct, practice or relationships shall constitute or otherwise be the basis of or entitle any person or class of persons to have or claim any minority status, quota preferences, protected status, or claim of discrimination.

Shawn, Daniel, Jim and their two friends went back to their party. Everyone could see they had a story to tell. "We jumped a fag," they said, "and threw him in the stream." The other kids laughed and pumped them for details, then resumed dancing and drinking.

Around 1 a.m., rescue divers pulled the body of Charlie Howard, 23, out of the Kenduskeag, a few hundred feet down-

stream from the bridge.

Daniel Ness turned himself in the next morning, as soon as he heard the news. He couldn't believe Charlie was dead. They never intended to kill anybody — they just meant to "show" him. Shawn Mabry and Jim Baines decided to hop a freight train out of town but had second thoughts when they got to the railroad tracks. They each went home, where they were arrested. All three spent Sunday night in the Hancock County Jail.

Local and state authorities agreed on Monday morning that the youths posed no further threat to the community. Shawn, Daniel and Jim were released into their

parents' custody. The state filed formal charges of murder the following week. The boys were later tried as juveniles rather than as adults. All three were convicted and sentenced to detention at the Maine Youth Center.

On the Monday night after Charlie Howard's murder, more than 200 people crowded into a memorial service at the Unitarian Church. Afterward, a candlelight procession crossed the bridge. Charlie's mother had requested that someone drop a white rose into the water. The marchers moved on to the main police station, where they stood silently in the street. Hecklers from the crowd of onlookers shouted obscene names.

A week later, at the spot on the bridge where Charlie Howard was tossed over, someone spray-painted three words: "Faggots Jump Here." ◆

Opposite page. Police divers searched the stream for Charlie Howard's body.

Left. In the days following the murder, the bridge became a focal point for Bangor residents' grief and outrage.

Street Justice

Immigrants to our country often face suspicion and prejudice from the established community. It's not uncommon for immigrant groups and other minorities to treat each other with a similar intolerance. Jewish merchants in California objected to the influx of Chinese competitors in the 1870s. Decades later, African Americans in Detroit gradually abandoned certain neighborhoods as Polish immigrants moved in.

The Crown Heights section of Brooklyn, N.Y., has experienced both the influx af immigrants and the exodus of many longtime residents. In the 1990s, it was a place that two strikingly different communities called home.

I N ANOTHER NEW YORK CITY neighborhood, 7-year-old Gavin Cato's death on the sidewalk by a runaway car might have seemed a random urban tragedy. But to many black residents of Crown Heights, the accident and its consequences made all too much sense.

The Cato family came to the United States in 1990 from the poor Caribbean country of Guyana. In Crown Heights, in the heart of Brooklyn, they found a crowded "island" of Caribbean immigrants, the fastest-growing segment of the local African American community. Voices and boom-boxes on the street sounded familiar. Corner grocery stores offered the tropical flavors of home. Gavin Cato loved to race his bicycle around the block, calling to his neighbors by the funny nicknames he gave them.

Not everyone in the neighborhood reminded Gavin and his family of the place they left behind. Since World War II, Crown Heights has also been home to an Orthodox Jewish community known as the Lubavitchers, who

A View from the Street

One black resident of Crown Heights observed:

We often say about Crown Heights and the neighborhood surrounding it that there are more West Indians living in Crown Heights in that part of Brooklyn than there are in the entire Caribbean. ... One thing that [is] immediately apparent to the new immigrant is that there is no public space that is shared between the Hasid and the West Indian community. ... I'm speaking about public transportation, public housing, public schools. ... Although we live in the same neighborhood right next to each other, we don't share these three public spaces. And I think that ... has proven to be the greatest obstacle to communication. ...

I was on the street that night ... and I mean you come out of the subway and you know something is wrong when you smell smoke; you see police cars speeding down the road, bands of young people with book bags on their back. And you think why do these young people have all these book bags on their back? It's late in the evening, school is over already. And then you realize those book bags have bottles and rocks.

fled Nazi persecution in Eastern Europe. The group makes up roughly 10 percent of the local population. While members of other white ethnic communities began leaving Crown Heights for the suburbs in the 1950s, the Lubavitchers stayed. Here their leaders had set up the movement's world headquarters. Loyalty to the neighborhood became a matter of faith.

Religious observance governs every aspect of Lubavitcher life, including diet and clothing. Long beards, long black coats and black hats give Lubavitcher men a distinctive appearance. The ancient laws and customs of Orthodox Judaism restrict social contact between Lubavitcher men and women and require separation of the sexes during worship. The group operates its own schools. A rule against using machinery on the Sabbath (Saturday) means that everyone must live within walking distance of the synagogue. The

Lubavitchers and their black neighbors live side by side but worlds apart.

On a hot August night in 1991, at the corner of President Street and Utica Avenue, these two worlds collided.

Gavin Cato and his cousin Angela, also 7, were playing outside their apartment building on the north side of President Street. It was after dark, but the sidewalk still gave off waves of warmth. At approximately 8:20, a 1984 Mercury Grand Marquis station wagon sped up to beat the changing traffic light at Utica. In the intersection it hit another car, then swerved out of control. Gavin and Angela heard the noise but couldn't move fast enough. The station wagon slammed them against the iron grate of a basement window.

Witnesses rushed to the site. People came out of nearby buildings. When Yosef Lifsch, the 22-year-old driver, got out of the Mercury, he tried to help unpin the children. But the crowd attacked

Yosef Lifsch got out of the Mercury and tried to help unpin the children. But the crowd attacked him.

An accident in the street unleashed the anger of a divided community.

Further Instructions

Fliers printed with the following message were distributed prior to a rally in Crown Heights on September 13, 1991.

NO JUSTICE NO PEACE

BLACK BROTHERS AND SISTERS UNITE AGAINST YOUR JEWISH BOSSES.

LISTEN TO WLIB FOR FURTHER INSTRUCTIONS.

SISTERS, BABY SITTERS AND HOUSEKEEPERS FOR JEWS, TAKE WHAT'S YOURS, LEAVE NO MARKS ON THE KID.

IN THE WORDS OF SONNY CARSON, DO WHAT HAS TO BE DONE.

FOOD PROCESSORS, DO WHAT JESSE DID, SPIT IN THEIR KOSHER FOOD.

FACTORY WORKERS, DAMAGE THEIR JEWISH GOODS.

STORE WORKERS, IT'S ALL YOURS.

REMEMBER MALCOLM X! FOREVER.

MAKE FIVE COPIES OF THIS AND GIVE IT TO YOUR PEOPLE.

him. Someone took his wallet. The wounds he received on his head and body would require 18 stitches.

Yosef Lifsch was a Lubavitcher. Official Lubavitcher business had brought him out that evening: to accompany Rabbi Menachem Schneerson on the Lubavitcher leader's weekly visit to his wife's grave. On the drive home from the cemetery, Lifsch's car was last in the procession, behind the Rabbi's. As usual, an unmarked 71st Precinct police car led the way.

The first two cars crossed the intersection, but Lifsch didn't make the green light. He sped on through to stay with the convoy and ran up onto a curb. Now two children lay bleeding on the pavement, and Lifsch was being beaten. Amid the confusion a black man knelt over Gavin Cato and began the strong, steady rhythm of CPR.

One of Lifsch's passengers, also a

Lubavitcher, attempted to call 911 from the car phone. Before he could finish dialing, someone stole the receiver. Strangers began punching him, pulling at his clothes. One black man grabbed him and called out, "He's mine! I'm going to have him arrested!"

The black man dragged the Lubavitcher clear of the turmoil. Then he let him go. "You owe me one," the black man said. He never gave his name.

The first official vehicle to reach the scene was an ambulance from the Hatzoloh Ambulance Service, a volunteer organization operated by the Orthodox Jewish community. (Hatzoloh means "rescue" in Hebrew.) A police car and a regular Emergency Medical Service ambulance arrived moments later. The two police officers opened a path through the throng, which had begun chanting "Jews! Jews! Jews!"

When one of the officers found Yosef Lifsch and two other Lubavitchers under attack, she intervened. In the interest of restoring order, the officer instructed the Hatzoloh driver to remove the three Jewish men from the area. Then the EMS paramedics reached Gavin Cato. To many black onlookers, something was clearly wrong with this sequence of events. Right away the rumor started — that the Jewish ambulance crew had refused to treat the injured black children.

For a long time, blacks in Crown Heights had observed what they considered preferential treatment by city officials toward the Lubavitchers. African American leaders charged that the Jewish minority had received undue government housing subsidies. A redistricting of the neighborhood's community boards in the 1970s was seen as giving Lubavitchers unfair political influence.

The Lubavitchers, on the other hand, contended that their minority status in Crown Heights, along with their distinctive practices, made them easy targets for bias crimes. Tensions between the two groups erupted in 1978 after members of a Lubavitcher anti-crime patrol severely assaulted a black teenager.

Black residents also cited a more routine pattern of inequities. Every Saturday, for instance, the police closed several major arteries to automobile traffic in order to accommodate the flow of Jewish pedestrians to and from Sabbath services. Black doctors with offices on these streets complained that the roadblocks forced even their sick and elderly patients to walk considerable distances. The Rabbi's police escort was seen as another example of favoritism. From this perspective, such special provisions made the latest allegation easy enough to believe.

Separate ambulances took Gavin and

Four days of violence in Crown Heights pitted neighbor against neighbor.

Angela Cato to Kings County Hospital. Gavin was pronounced dead within minutes, and doctors classified Angela's condition as critical.

New details and rumors traveled quickly. As one story had it, the police beat Gavin Cato's father as he tried to lift the station wagon off his son. People asked why the Jewish driver hadn't been arrested. Word spread that Rabbi Schneerson himself was the driver, and even that he had fled the scene.

Back on President Street, the Police Department Accident Squad hooked up floodlights to mark the site. The bright glow attracted even more attention. Up and down the block, blacks and Lubavitchers got into shouting matches, trading racial slurs. According to eyewitnesses, 15 to 20 police officers watched while black youths started throwing bottles and stones at cars and buildings and the few Lubavitchers who remained on the street. Some of the assailants reportedly chanted, "The Jews killed the kids!"

As tension mounted, the officers, too, became targets of attack. One black man was arrested for firing a .357-caliber Magnum at the police and another for pelting the crowd with a slingshot. At least a dozen officers were injured by objects hurled from nearby roofs.

"It was fun, throwing bottles at the cops," a 13-year-old later told a reporter. Other young people said that the outbreak offered something to do on a hot night besides hanging out or watching TV.

Alarm bells sounded around the neighborhood as scattered rioters turned to looting stores. Nearly 100 bystanders watched some young men force open the security gate at Sneaker King. The looters smashed windows and grabbed armfuls of shoes and T-shirts inside. A similar break-in at the Utica Gold Exchange resulted in a fire. Several Korean- and Iranian-owned businesses, in addition to those owned by Jews, suffered serious damage.

Adequate police support was slow to arrive. When the disturbance began, more than 100 officers of the 71st Precinct — including

> *They started cursing him and yelling, "Kill the Jew!" One of them thrust a knife blade four times into the man's left side.*

the new Commanding Officer, Capt. Vincent Kennedy — were on security assignment at a nearby B.B. King concert. Notified by radio, Capt. Kennedy drove to the scene and promptly summoned 30 officers and three sergeants from the concert detail.

Over the next two hours, some 350 officers converged on Crown Heights. Kennedy set up a temporary command post on Eastern Parkway and ordered the barricading of the Lubavitcher Headquarters, two blocks to the east. His other zone of concentration was the commercial area around the accident site. The remainder of the forces fanned out across 30 square blocks.

At 11 o'clock, people still filled the streets. When the B.B. King concert ended, hundreds more black youths made their way to the intersection of President and Utica. They saw a police truck towing Yosef Lifsch's station wagon off the sidewalk, revealing a splotch of blood. A tall man jumped up onto a car and shouted: "Do you feel what I feel? Do you feel the pain? What are you going to do about it? Let's take Kingston Avenue!"

His listeners began to move. Along President Street, the mostly teenage crowd smashed the windows of cars and businesses and homes thought to be Jewish-owned. (Some of the cars the rioters overturned or burned actually belonged to black families.) Blacks in Crown Heights had long accused the Lubavitchers of trying to buy up the neighborhood. The mood that night brought this smoldering resentment to a flame.

"Arrest the Jews!" young black men and women called out. "Heil, Hitler!" Some of them carried school backpacks loaded with bottles and bricks.

Small groups broke off from the main mob and roamed the neighborhood. "You want to see how strong the black man is?" yelled one youth as he helped flip a police car. "It made me feel like I scored a point," another participant later explained. On Carroll Street, 15 youths attacked a 32-year-old Jewish man with a hail of rocks and bottles. "Jews, get out of here!" they chanted as they kicked him. Nearby, another Jewish man was assaulted and robbed.

At the corner of President Street and Brooklyn Avenue, three blocks from the accident and three hours after it occurred, some teenagers stopped a car. They could tell the driver was Jewish by his hat and beard. They started cursing him and yelling, "Kill the Jew!" Yankel Rosenbaum jumped out of the car. The youths closed in, and one of them thrust a knife blade four times into the man's left side. He slumped over on the hood. When a police car showed up, the young men scattered and left him bleeding.

Within a few minutes of the stabbing, the police arrested a 16-year-old black youth named Lemrick Nelson and charged him with the crime. At the time of the arrest, Nelson was reportedly carrying a bloody knife in his pocket. According to neighbors, he had recently spray-painted a swastika in the lobby of his apartment building after a dispute with the Jewish landlord.

Yankel Rosenbaum died at Kings County Hospital three hours after he was attacked. The 29-year-old Orthodox Jewish scholar had been visiting from Australia. He was not a Lubavitcher but lived in the home of some friends in the community. He spent most of his waking hours in the libraries and archives of Manhattan, conducting research on the persecution of Jews in the Holocaust. Rosenbaum's parents had survived the Holocaust in Poland.

A state court jury acquitted Lemrick Nelson of criminal charges in 1992. Protests by the Hasidic community, and political pressure from a variety of sources, led to a U.S. Justice Department review of the case. In August 1994, Nelson was indicted on federal charges that he violated Yankel Rosenbaum's civil rights. ◆

Heard It Through the Grapevine

Rumors travel fast. Imagine being at the mall. You see a tall guy in the food court and think it may be Michael Jordan. He disappears. You tell some friends you run into, and one of them says it makes sense — there's a celebrity golf tournament in town this weekend. A store clerk partially overhears your conversation and alerts her co-workers. Two minutes later, the crowd gathered near the fountain surges toward the tall man as he steps out of the restroom. He isn't Michael Jordan.

Occasionally, rumors turn out to be true. But what makes them rumors to start with is the absence of proof. So why do they spread like wildfire, and why do we believe them?

Sometimes our wishes can play tricks on our eyes. And the same desires in others can make our claims believable. Take the Michael Jordan example. Michael wasn't at the mall, but someone who resembled him was. A longer look at that person might have prevented the rumor, but a brief glimpse was proof enough for a Jordan fan. Favorable circumstances — the celebrity golf tournament, for instance — can quickly dissolve all doubt.

Often the force driving a rumor is not desire but fear. A friend claims that his cousin found a mouse floating in her soda can. By repeating such a story, people

attempt to prove that big industry can't be trusted.

Some rumors reflect prejudices and help to justify them. Immediately after the 1995 bombing of the Federal Building in Oklahoma City, reports circulated that three men of "Middle Eastern origin" had been spotted leaving the scene. Long after the rumor proved false, some people continued using it to harass Arab Americans.

Under special circumstances, such as elections or wars or natural disasters, rumors seem to flourish. Riots are another of these breeding grounds. Tension and confusion make people scramble for explanations of what's going on. Falsehoods can sometimes be simpler than the truth, and thus more useful in making quick

sense out of chaos.

In Crown Heights, one rumor accused a Jewish ambulance crew of ignoring two injured black children. According to another, the police beat a black father as he tried to rescue his son. Still a third placed the Jewish community's spiritual leader behind the wheel of the runaway vehicle.

None of these rumors was true, but grief and fear and rage made them irresistible. Like a cry of "Fire!" in a crowded theater, these messages didn't take much explaining. They painted the Lubavitchers and the police as demons. They touched off more explosions of anger. Before the rumors burned out, another innocent person had died.

Out of the Shadows

Although this book has focused on our nation's past, it is our present and future that most concern us all. Change is a slow and often painful process, but we have made astonishing headway in the last few decades. Attitudes have changed, opportunities have expanded, in ways that no one could have imagined in the days of Jim Crow. We are a more open, more accepting, more tolerant society than we were 30 years ago.

Yet intolerance and violence are still woven into the fabric of American life. Klanwatch, a project of the Southern Poverty Law Center, documented 108 bias-motivated murders between 1990 and 1993, as well as thousands of assaults, cross-burnings and acts of arson and intimidation. Ku Klux Klan, Neo-Nazi and Skinhead organizations operate in every state of the union. In 1994, there were more than 300 hate groups scattered throughout the United States.

Not all bigots join hate groups, however, and not all bias-motivated violence is committed by those who shave their heads or wear hoods. In the last few years there has been a dismaying rise in the number of bias crimes committed by young Americans — such as the ones who killed Charlie Howard — who have no affiliation with any organized movement.

Equally troubling is the willingness of so many people to look the other way. In a 1992 survey of high school students, 30 percent said they would participate in racist incidents, and 17 percent said they would silently support them. These numbers suggest that we still have much to learn from the bitter harvests of our past — that our democracy is still a work in progress.

Though as a nation we have often failed to acknowledge it, our strength has always arisen from our diversity. America's great achievements — in art, in literature, in science and government — have come about because we were open to new peoples, new ideas, new visions. Throughout our history, individuals and groups have made great sacrifices for the cause of freedom and equality. Their example can inspire us to learn to live together in harmony.

We can, as Martin Luther King Jr. said, rise up and live out the true meaning of our creed. But only if we confront the shadows of our past. Only if we overcome the temptation to deny or diminish the humanity of our neighbors. Only if we affirm that, whatever our differences, "We the people" are one.

FURTHER READING

Ashabrunner, Brent. *Still a Nation of Immigrants*. New York: Cobblehill Books, 1993.

Blumenfeld, Warren, and Diane Raymond. *Looking at Gay and Lesbian Life*. Boston: Beacon Press, 1993.

Brown, Dee. *Bury My Heart at Wounded Knee: An Indian History of the American West*. New York: Henry Holt & Co., 1991.

Calloway, Colin G., ed. *The World Turned Upside Down: Indian Voices from Early America*. Boston: Bedford Books, 1994.

Daniels, Roger. *Prisoners Without Trial: Japanese Americans in World War II*. New York: Hill and Wang, 1993.

De Leon, Arnoldo. *They Called Them Greasers*. Austin: University of Texas Press, 1983.

Dinnerstein, Leo. *The Leo Frank Case*. Athens, Ga.: Brown Thrasher Books, 1987.

————. *Uneasy at Home: Anti-Semitism and the American Jewish Experience*. New York: Columbia University Press, 1987.

Emsden, Katharine, ed. *Coming to America: A New Life in a New Land*. Lowell, Mass.: Discovery Enterprises, Ltd., 1993.

Gould, Stephen Jay. *The Mismeasure of Man*. New York: W.W. Norton & Co., 1981.

Greene, Bette. *The Drowning of Stephan Jones*. New York: Bantam, 1991.

Hamm, Mark S. *American Skinheads: The Criminology and Control of Hate Crimes*. Westport, Conn.: Praeger, 1993.

Hansen, Ellen, ed. *The Underground Railroad: Life on the Road to Freedom*. Lowell, Mass.: Discovery Enterprises, Ltd., 1993.

Hongo, Florence M., et al. *Japanese American Journey*. San Mateo, Cal.: Japanese American Curriculum Project, 1985.

Jacobs, Harriet A. *Incidents in the Life of a Slave Girl, Written by Herself*. Jean Fagan Yellin, ed. Cambridge, Mass.: Harvard University Press, 1987.

Katz, Jonathan Ned. *Gay American History*. New York: Meridian, 1992.

Kennedy, Stetson. *Jim Crow Guide*. Gainesville: University Press of Florida, 1992.

LeSueur, Stephen C. *The 1838 Mormon War in Missouri*. Columbia, Mo.: University of Missouri Press, 1987.

Loewen, James, W. *Lies My Teacher Told Me: Everything Your American History Textbook Got Wrong*. New York: The New Press, 1995.

Lyons, Mary E. *Letters from a Slave Girl*. New York: Charles Scribner's Sons, 1992.

McWilliams, Carey, and Matt S. Meier. *North from Mexico: The Spanish-Speaking People of the United States*. New York: Praeger, 1990.

Meyers, Madeleine, ed. *The Cherokee Nation: Life Before the Tears*. Lowell, Mass.: Discovery Enterprises, Ltd., 1994.

Montejano, David. *Anglos and Mexicans in the Making of Texas, 1836-1986*. Austin: University of Texas Press, 1987.

Newton, Michael and Judy Ann. *The Ku Klux Klan: An Encyclopedia*. New York: Garland, 1991.

Northup, Solomon. *Twelve Years a Slave*. Sue Eakin and Joseph Logsdon, eds. Baton Rouge: Louisiana State University Press, 1968.

Perlmutter, Philip. *Divided We Fall: A History of Ethnic, Religious, and Racial Prejudice in America*. Ames: Iowa State University Press, 1992.

Stepto, Michelle, ed. *Our Song, Our Toil: The Story of American Slavery as Told by Slaves*. Brookfield, Conn.: Millbrook Press, 1994.

Storti, Craig. *Incident at Bitter Creek*. Ames: Iowa State University Press, 1991.

Takaki, Ronald. *Issei and Nisei: The Settling of Japanese America*. New York: Chelsea House, 1989.

————. *Journey to Gold Mountain: The Chinese in 19th-Century America*. New York: Chelsea House, 1994.

Trask, Richard B. *Salem Village and the Witch Hysteria*. Amawalk, N.Y.: Jackdaw Publications, 1993.

Weber, David J., ed. *Foreigners in Their Native Land: Historical Roots of the Mexican Americans*. Albuquerque: University of New Mexico Press, 1992.

Williams, Jeanne. *Trails of Tears: American Indians Driven from Their Lands*. Dallas: Hendrick-Long Publishing Co., 1992.

Woog, Dan. *School's Out: The Impact of Gay and Lesbian Issues on America's Schools*. Boston: Alyson Publications, 1995.

Wormser, Richard. *American Islam: Growing Up Muslim in America*. New York: Walker and Co., 1994.

Zinn, Howard. *A People's History of the United States*. New York: HarperCollins, 1990.

ACKNOWLEDGMENTS

This book was produced by Teaching Tolerance, a project of the Southern Poverty Law Center. The editor was Sara Bullard. The design director was Art Dees. Manuscript editors were David Aronson, Elsie Williams, Glenda Valentine, Houston Roberson and Richard Cohen. The photo researcher was Glenda Valentine. Special thanks to David Aronson, who contributed the Rosewood story.

Grateful acknowledgment is made to the following individuals and organizations: Jennifer Gruber, Jessica Cohen, Charles Guggenheim, the state archives of California, Florida, Massachusetts, North Carolina, Oklahoma and Texas, Barker American History Center, Benson Latin American Collection, Boston Public Library, Free Library of Philadelphia, Los Angeles County Library, UCLA Research Library, Rock Springs (Wyo.) Public Library, Bangor (Maine) Public Library, New York State Division of Criminal Justice Services, Anti-Defamation League of B'nai B'rith, Klanwatch, The Boston Phoenix, Scott Prentzas, Sox Kitashima, Bette Greene, Lois Reed, Kevin Berrill, Warren Blumenfeld, Martin Duberman, Rebecca Lovejoy, Sophia Seals, Tom Kreneck, Henry Hottmann, Tiger Knowles, Pat Louis, Erin Kellen, John Wunder, Paul Fees, Ada Bauman, Margaret McKinnon and Bill Welge.

Teaching Tolerance was founded in 1991 to provide teachers with resources and ideas to help promote harmony in the classroom. The Southern Poverty Law Center is a nonprofit legal and education foundation based in Montgomery, Alabama. The Center's Executive Chairman is Morris Dees. Its Executive Director is Edward Ashworth. Its directors are Joseph J. Levin, Jr., Patricia Clark, Frances Green, Hon. Rufus Huffman, Howard Mandell and Jack Watson.

PICTURE CREDITS

Front cover, clockwise from top left: Library of Congress; Library of Congress; Jim West, Impact Visuals; *Los Angeles Times* photo; National Archives.
Frontispiece: Library of Congress.
3: Collection of the Supreme Court of the United States.
4-5: Yale University Art Gallery.
8-12: Stock Montage.
16: Stock Montage.
17-18: Western History Collections, University of Oklahoma.
21: adapted from *Atlas of the North American Indian.*
24-25: (top) Archive Photos (# 289.3); (bottom) Archives, Reorganized Church of Jesus Christ of Latter Day Saints.
26: Archives, Reorganized Church of Jesus Christ of Latter Day Saints.
27: (top) Historical Department, Church of Jesus Christ of Latter-Day Saints; (bottom) "Haun's Mill" by C. C. A. Christensen, Courtesy Museum of Art, Brigham Young University.
28: Stock Montage.
32: "Land of the Free and Home of the Brave" by Henry Byam Martin, Courtesy National Archives of Canada, Ottawa (# C-115001).
34-36: Collection of The New-York Historical Society.
38: Courtesy Harvard University Press.
39: (top) Leonard Freed/Magnum; (bottom) Library of Congress (# LC-USF33-30577-M2).
42: Boston Athenaeum.
44: The Library Company of Philadelphia.
45: The Granger Collection, New York.
46: The Library Company of Philadelphia.
50-51: (left) Visual Communications; (right) Denver Public Library, Western History Department.
52: Sweetwater County (Wyo.) Historical Museum.
53: Stock Montage.
54: Special Collections Division, University of Washington Libraries (# UW8679).
55: (top) Library of Congress (# LC-USZ62-27755); (bottom) Courtesy The Bancroft Library.
56: Union Pacific Museum Collection.
57: Sweetwater County (Wyo.) Historical Museum.
61: Buffalo Bill Historical Center, Cody, Wyo., Vincent Mercaldo Collection.
62-63: (top left) Smithsonian Institution (# 3195-A); (top right and bottom) Nebraska State Historical Society.
64: (top) Smithsonian Institution (# 3200-B-2); (bottom) Nebraska State Historical Society.
65: Bettmann Archive.
68-71: Atlanta History Center.
74-75: (left) Atlanta History Center; (center and right) Anti-Defamation League.
78: The Institute of Texan Cultures, San Antonio.
79: Western History Collections, University of Oklahoma.
80: Benson Latin American Collection, University of Texas at Austin.
81: Dr. Hector P. Garcia Papers, Special Collections and Archives Dept., Texas A & M University-Corpus Christi Library.
82: Archives Division, Texas State Library.
83: Russell Lee Photograph Collection, Center for American History, University of Texas at Austin (# CN 07207).
86-87: Florida State Archives.
88: Western History Collections, University of Oklahoma.
90-91: (bottom) University of Tulsa Special Collections, Tulsa Race Riots 1921 Papers; (top) Florida State Archives.
94: Courtesy Sox Kitashima.
95-99: National Archives.
101: Visual Communications.
104-107: Klanwatch.
108: Stock Montage.
109: Klanwatch.
110: *Mobile Press Register.*
111: Gilles Peres.
113: Courtesy Lois Reed.
114: Photo by Tracy Baim/Outlines-Chicago.
116-117: (top left and bottom) Donna Binder, Impact Visuals; (top right) Jim West, Impact Visuals.
118-119: *Bangor Daily News.*
122-125: *Newsday*/J. Paraskevas.
Back cover, left to right: Anti-Defamation League; National Japanese American Historical Society; Center for American History, the University of Texas at Austin.

INDEX

Jim Carnes was born in Columbus, Mississippi, in 1955. After graduating from the University of North Carolina at Chapel Hill, he served as an editor with *Encyclopaedia Britannica* for eight years. He is currently a senior writer with the Teaching Tolerance project of the Southern Poverty Law Center in Montgomery, Alabama.

Harry A. Blackmun served as an Associate Justice of the United States Supreme Court from 1970 until 1994. He has received more than 30 honorary degrees and numerous awards, including the American Liberties Medallion, presented by the American Jewish Committee, and the Public Service Award of the Aspen Institute for Humanistic Studies. Justice Blackmun speaks frequently on the topics of racism and intolerance.

The Teaching Tolerance project, introduced by the Southern Poverty Law Center in 1991, provides teachers of all grade levels with practical classroom resources to help them foster unity, respect, and equality in the classroom. Through the generous support of the Center's donors, all Teaching Tolerance materials are made available free or at minimal cost to educators nationwide.

The cornerstone of the project is a semiannual magazine, *Teaching Tolerance*, that is mailed to more than 500,000 teachers in 50 states and more than a dozen foreign countries. EdPress (Educational Press Association) awarded the magazine its highest honor, the Golden Lamp, in 1995.

In January 1992, Teaching Tolerance released *America's Civil Rights Movement*, a teaching kit comprising *A Time for Justice*, a 38-minute documentary video on the history of the movement; the text *Free at Last: A History of the Civil Rights Movement and Those Who Died in the Struggle;* and a teacher's guide. Targeted at secondary students, the *Civil Rights* kit has been distributed to more than 50,000 schools. *A Time for Justice* received the 1995 Academy Award for best short documentary.

In March 1995, Teaching Tolerance released its second video and text package, *The Shadow of Hate,* of which *Us and Them* is the text component. This kit, examining the history of intolerance in America, also includes a 40-minute video, *The Shadow of Hate,* and a teacher's guide.

For more information on the Teaching Tolerance program, contact:

Teaching Tolerance
400 Washington Avenue
Montgomery, AL 36104
Phone (334) 264-0286
Fax (334) 264-3121